THE
APOLOGY

THE APOLOGY

EVE ENSLER

BLOOMSBURY PUBLISHING

NEW YORK · LONDON · OXFORD · NEW DELHI · SYDNEY

BLOOMSBURY PUBLISHING
Bloomsbury Publishing Inc.
1385 Broadway, New York, NY 10018, USA

BLOOMSBURY, BLOOMSBURY PUBLISHING, and the Diana logo are
trademarks of Bloomsbury Publishing Plc

First published in the United States 2019

ISBN: HB: 978-1-63557-438-8; eBook: 978-1-63557-439-5

Library of Congress Cataloging-in-Publication Data is available

2 4 6 8 10 9 7 5 3 1

Typeset by Westchester Publishing Services

Printed and bound in the U.S.A. by Berryville Graphics Inc., Berryville, Virginia

To find out more about our authors and books visit www.bloomsbury.com
and sign up for our newsletters.

Bloomsbury books may be purchased for business or promotional use. For
information on bulk purchases please contact Macmillan Corporate and
Premium Sales Department at specialmarkets@macmillan.com.

FOR EVERY WOMAN STILL WAITING

FOR AN APOLOGY

I am done waiting. My father is long dead. He will never say the words to me. He will not make the apology. So it must be imagined. For it is in our imagination that we can dream across boundaries, deepen the narrative, and design alternative outcomes.

This letter is an invocation, a calling up. I have tried to allow my father to speak to me as he would speak. Although I have written the words I needed my father to say to me, I had to make space for him to come through me.

There is so much about him, his history, that he never shared with me, so I have had to conjure much of that as well.

This letter is my attempt to endow my father with the will and the words to cross the border, and speak the language, of apology so that I can finally be free.

DEAR EVIE,

How very strange to be writing you. Am I writing to you from the grave or the past or the future? Am I writing as you or as you would like me to be or as I really am beneath my own limited understanding? And does it matter? Am I writing in a language I never spoke or understood which you have created inside both of our minds to bridge the gaps, the failures to connect? Maybe I am writing as I truly am, as you have freed me by your witness. Or I'm not writing this at all but simply being used as a vehicle to fulfill your own needs and version of things.

I don't remember ever writing you a letter. I rarely wrote letters. For me to write a letter, to reach out to others, would have been a sign of weakness. People wrote letters to me. I would never let anyone know they were significant enough to me to write a letter to them. That would make me less, put me at a disadvantage. Even saying this to you feels odd. This is not something I would normally know or say unless you had entered my mind. But I would not argue with it. It feels true.

You always wrote me letters. I found that peculiar and strangely moving. We lived in the same house but you were writing to me, your little-girl handwriting attempting straight lines but wandering all over the page. It was as if you were trying to make contact with some aspect of me, a part you could not find in the heated moments of our conflict, as if you were trying through poetry to appeal to a secret self that I had once made available to you. Usually you wrote apology letters. So fitting that you would now want an apology letter from me. You were always apologizing, begging for forgiveness. I had reduced you to a daily degrading mantra of "I'm sorry."

Once I sent you to your room without dinner and made you stay there as long as it took for you to understand and admit to your bad behavior. You were initially stubborn, quiet for twenty-four hours. Your mother was worried. But then you must have gotten hungry or bored. You wrote me a letter on a piece of cardboard that came from the dry cleaner with my shirts. You slipped it under my bedroom door. It was a dramatic plea. It was a list.

You were always big on lists. I see now you needed to catalog things, make sense in a kind of literary arithmetic.

It was a list of what you had learned and what you would never do again. I remember that lying was number one. You would never lie again. And I knew even as I hounded you daily and made you believe you were a despicable liar that you were the most honest little girl I ever knew, although I did not know many little girls. I despised children. They were loud and messy and misbehaved. I was way too old to have children and I only had them to carry on my legacy. But I digress. That cardboard letter with your urgent writing in purple Magic Marker and the lopsided flowers you drew on the edges got you out of the room, and I wonder now if that is why you continued to write, as a kind of passport to freedom.

Since I left the world of the living I have been stuck in a most debilitating zone. It is very much what people describe when they talk about limbo: a void, oblivion. Limbo, not an external place exactly. To the contrary, I have been essentially nowhere. Floating, unmoored, spinning. There is nothing here, nothing to see, no trees, no ocean, no sounds or smells, no light. There is no place as you know place, no rooting, nothing to hold on to. No, nothing but the reflection of what lives inside me.

"What is hell? Hell is oneself."

That is Eliot. You may not know that he was my favorite poet. His words come to me often in this limbo. I have been spiraling here for almost thirty-one years in your time, but it is odd as there is no time where I am. There is just an agonizing emptiness, endless swallowing space that is at once terrifyingly vast and utterly claustrophobic.

I left the world of the living with so many resentments and grudges. Even on my deathbed, the virulence of my wrath was more powerful than the cancer that consumed my body. My rage was so pernicious it was able to fight through the morphine and the delirium and fuel me to design and enact my final punishments. And your poor mother. What was she to do? I had terrorized her for so many years, battering her with my loudness, condescension, and threats that she was by then a cowed and devoted accomplice. She tried to humor me. She told me this might not be the moment to make such extreme decisions. She did everything but tell me I had lost my mind.

My very last thoughts and breaths were suffused with a desire to hurt, a desire to create long-lasting suffering.

Perhaps you do not know this, but at that final moment, I insisted she strike you from my will. You would inherit nothing. "Nothing!" I said it with great force. Even in my very weakened state this vengeance gave me life. It was my last chance at abolishing you, eradicating you, punishing you.

And when your mother asked me to reconsider, I insisted that you had brought this on yourself. Why would I leave anything to a child who had been so obstinate and disloyal? Your mother's challenging me enraged me further and I became more vindictive, attempting to erase even your character. I forced her to promise me that no matter what you told her after I was gone, she would never believe you, as it was well established many years earlier that you were a bald-faced liar. Liar. I forced your mother to commit to essentially distrusting and doubting you forever. In that sense I forced her to kill you off as I had killed you off. I forced her to choose her husband over her daughter. But this was not new. She was well practiced in that sacrifice. I had demanded this of her for most of your life. And I knew, I truly knew how much she despised herself for agreeing. I saw the way I had, over the years, eroded her self-respect as a mother, erased her confidence and voice, made her feel weak until she was no longer likable or remotely recognizable to herself, and yet I had still insisted.

I spent the first of what felt like years in this death realm in an endless loop of all the betrayals and disappointments, all the ways colleagues and children and so-called friends had enacted their stupidity or weakness, replaying each justifiable antipathy and exacting imagined revenge. Of course, you were high on the list.

I left the world so furious with you that I punished you by refusing even to let you know I was dying. I would not call to say goodbye. I wanted you to be cut and bleeding with the shards of my rage, so you would be forced to carry me around, hemorrhaging with guilt and despair, questioning for the rest of your life why you never measured up, never became the daughter I expected you to be.

Intent on leaving you without closure or finality, I didn't even plan or allow for a memorial or a funeral. I found them to be pedestrian and pathetic displays of nonsense and useless emotion. And furthermore, if you mourned me, there was the very likely possibility that you would release me. Withholding was the only power I had at that point, the only way to seize your being, the only way to get your attention and keep your attention.

A few days after I died, before I entered this realm, I spied you sitting on the floor of my closet in Florida, my old yellow cashmere sweater pressed against your face. At first I did not understand what you were doing, but then as I studied you, I realized you were smelling me, the residue of me, inhaling my cologne and essence, trying to find a place to harbor your grief. And despite myself, this touched me. It brought me back to a time that was soft between us, a time sheltered by an almost unbearable affection. You, on the floor of my closet, trying to find me, to find that tenderness, sparked in me a wave of sorrow and loss—and then I was gone. Gone from your world, gone from beauty, gone from the possibility of salvation. Thrown into the rampant rehashing of offenses and grievances.

They say as you live you shall die. And it's true that over time my fury became lethal. "Anger is a poison you mix for your friend but drink yourself," my mother would warn me, as I was always inexplicably angry. And then my rage turned, my whole system rotten and suffusing odious dread. It was as if the wrath had turned in on itself, devouring and suffocating my anguished psyche in an alley of regrets, excruciating anxiety, piercing doubts, torturous self-recrimination. There was no forward motion. There was no back. There was no way out. I had neither the language nor will nor understanding to get free, paralyzed in this zone of limbo.

I know I was a cynic who pooh-poohed the hogwash of an afterlife. But what did I really know about anything? And I wouldn't even call this an afterlife. It's not after anything but a continuation of. In that sense, death is agonizing and endless. Or perhaps this death, which has been specific to me. I imagine others are winged by their good purpose to more radiant zones.

If I have learned anything here, and it has been hard to learn much as my brain is addled with angst, what I have discovered is that it is critical to resolve conflicts while you are alive, as all unfinished business follows you into the next realm and determines your state of being. Each wrong you've caused in your life, each harm you have not taken responsibility for, becomes a kind of spiritual goo, a viscous substance that constructs your confinement. It's a cage, but it's inside you, and that is even more impossible and distressing. You are stuck into yourself, sucked down in the muck of eternal self-obsession. You would be screaming but the sludge is too thick to allow a voice. There is no respite.

So, thank you, Eve, for summoning me, giving me this opportunity to reckon with my horrific acts. I understand there are no guarantees that I will be released from this agonizing limbo, but your offer to receive this apology has already shifted this desperate landscape.

I realize you are clear in your purpose. The depth and sincerity and need of your mission are evident and powerful. I understand you are asking me to make an apology. I must say this is foreign and unnatural terrain for me. I don't remember ever apologizing for anything. In fact, it was drilled into me that to apologize was to expose weakness, to lay yourself vulnerable.

I imagine my vulnerability is in fact exactly what you need from me. Perhaps it was always what you needed. I will do my best to neither justify nor rationalize my actions. I will instead attempt to make an accounting of my actions and my intentions. The telling is not meant to elicit understanding or forgiveness. It is a confession in the deepest sense. It is unquestionably something I would prefer remain hidden from you, from God, from myself. But this is the moment when I give myself without reservation, without justification, to this reckoning.

I have asked myself, What is an apology? It is a humbling. It is an admission of wrongdoings and a surrender. It is an act of intimacy and connection which requires great self-knowledge and insight. I will most certainly come up short.

This apology required time. It could not be rushed. Fortunately I have had practice here endlessly reliving and rehashing my crimes, mentally reenacting the details. I know you have said that an apology must be thorough and can only be trusted in its veracity and dedication to details. I have done my best. I have followed your very strict guidelines: Recognize what I have done as a crime. Face how deeply my actions and violations have impacted and devastated you. See you as a human being. Attempt to experience or feel what it felt like inside you. Feel profound remorse and regret over my actions. And finally, take responsibility for my actions by doing extensive work to understand what made me do what I did.

I will need to go back in this letter to locate the roots of my behavior. I will be as honest as a formerly disingenuous person can be. I will attempt to proceed with neither defensiveness nor self-pity, as I understand neither will further clarify nor resolve.

Many of the living do not believe they are in relationship with the dead. I was one of them, hiding in the delusion, or perhaps the hope, that what is gone is gone. That we pass through as flesh-and-blood creatures and die and rot or are burned into ether.

The dead are yearning for the living. It is only through the living, through their deepest imaginings and empathy, that the dead can be known to themselves and can be freed. And if the living are able and willing to access their love of the dead, able to access their anger at the dead, essentially to be in relationship and true dialogue with the dead, the dead will rise and speak. We remain lodged and hidden inside our families and loved ones, those we have harmed and those we have fostered. We are there inside the walls of the old houses and the silence of the evening, inside the celebratory moments, the rites and rituals of births and weddings and funerals and any place where the living long for the witness and approbation of the dead. We are there like a dormant cell in the bloodstream, waiting to be catalyzed by the devotion of the living, by the need of the living to understand and have resolution. There, ignited by the generosity of the living to remember and cherish and argue and wrestle and restore.

It does not surprise me that it is you, Evie, who summoned me back. You, who were willing and able to hold my sorrow and grief when I could not venture near it, to weep my tears when I was dry, to claim and hold and attempt to know the essence of a soul I had betrayed.

I am sure it must surprise you to see that I can write, and even more to discover how I write, the language I speak. Frankly, it has surprised me. I imagine it is more formal and emotional than you would have predicted. But what you don't know (or perhaps deep inside you do), is that I dreamed of being a writer. A writer or a rabbi. I dreamed of a solitary life of meditation and study and reflection, a life of philosophy and grasping at the huge questions of meaning and matter.

I dreamed in many ways of the life you have lived. And if I take any solace in contemplating the consequences of my deplorable deeds, I sometimes imagine that perhaps it was my unfulfilled dreams that entered you and inspired your destiny. This is not an attempt to take credit for who you are or what you've become. You've made your life, every hard inch of it. And I know that so much of who you are was not so much about constructing but reconstructing, piecing back the fragments of self that I forcibly and strategically (whether consciously or not) splintered and disassembled. I am all too tragically aware of who you would have been—confident, secure in your memory and intelligence, happy, living inside your body. I saw who you were before I worked my destruction.

And perhaps that is why I had to hurt you so badly, hobble you at the knees from the beginning. There was no way I was going to let you go beyond me, show me up as the fraud or failure I was. But perhaps, just maybe, a piece of my true yearning was passed on to you. Did you know I dreamed of studying the Torah? It was my greatest ambition to give my whole self to that text, to sacrifice to it even my life.

I had no longing for children or a wife, which is why I did not marry until I was fifty. I held out as long as I could in hopes that some miraculous intervention would shift my path, grant me the dream of a life that lay buried beneath this one. I had very little interest in people. They annoyed me and disappointed me, whereas books and ideas were food and inspiration. I was at heart a recluse and a seeker forced into a 1950s household with a Midwestern wife, three children, an olive-green Cadillac, and a Popsicle company to run. How absurd!

So, thank you. Your call and your presence have interrupted the spinning, and for the first time in thirty-one years, the pain and the torture have paused. For that, even if it is only momentary, I am profoundly grateful. How odd. I was never grateful. I don't remember ever saying that word. Why would I be grateful when all the world was rightfully endowed to me? On the contrary, the world needed to be grateful for my existence.

My entitlement, the divine right of kings, was endowed by my mother, who by all accounts was an equally present, formidable, and reliable authority as God. She was very beautiful and very strict.

I was the youngest child, born much later than the others, clearly not planned but determinedly special. I was the accident that became the miracle. The golden child. The chosen one. The boy who would fulfill the promise of my mother's highest aspirations and relieve my father of his chronic depression and disappointment. From the time I was conscious, I was made to believe I was better, smarter, more precious, more deserving than anyone around me. What I didn't know was why. I still don't.

What I knew instinctively is that my mother's overwhelming need for this to be true had as much to do with her as it did with me. To deny it or contradict it would have called her fragilely assembled being into question and thrown my mother into despair.

I was her salvation. My arrival heralded the time of rising fortune. My mere existence would somehow resurrect her miserable marriage and redeem her suffering. I was light. I was darling. I was savior son. There is a kind of implicit hierarchy in adoration. The idolized one is above you, beyond you. And so I was lonely. Excruciatingly lonely. The loneliness of the adored.

You are separated out from the beginning as special. You are there to serve the need of the person who adores you, the person who has made you into the adored object. And I was indeed an object. My mother's adoration of me seemed to distance her from the object of her adoration, as if to touch me would diminish me. As if to treat me as a human would make me human. I don't remember her ever holding me or cuddling me. I don't remember her playing with me, chasing me, running on the green grass with me. I remember her directing me, correcting me, managing me, teaching me, shaping and constructing me. I ceased to be the subject of my life, rarely being allowed to feel sad or cry or misbehave.

My father, Hyman, was Austrian, and my mother, Sarah, was German. Both had been raised with the severest discipline. They were devotees of the practices of a well-known and highly popular German physician, Dr. Daniel Gottlob Moritz Schreber. Dr. Schreber strongly believed that babies should be taught from the outset to obey and should refrain from crying. The way to control a baby, he taught, was by frightening it, and after you would be master of the child forever. He strongly urged parents to refrain from physical demonstrations of affection like embracing, cuddling, or kissing.

The theory was that through withholding affection and inflicting terror and humiliation, children would obey authority figures and be deterred from acting from their own will. There were strict and detailed rules. The child would follow these and, like a wandering plant secured to a trellis, grow straight upward, climbing to the pinnacle of social and economic achievement and power.

Neither my mother nor father tolerated any digressions from their plans for me. As so many of their hopes rested with me, they were more severe with me than with their other children. I was their project. I was to be molded and perfected. My every move was monitored. You might say my mother was withholding or cold, but adulation is a powerful offering, an aphrodisiac. It fills you with a wildly enhanced version of yourself, charging you with a much-distorted and overblown confidence, an aggressive overdrive that never rests.

And inside, throughout all this, I felt plain, uninspired, and empty. But while my mother idealized me, my father saw me as lazy, pampered, unmotivated, coasting, unfocused, a loser of sorts. I felt much more aligned with his version of me. This would explain my endless anger. The divide between my mother's version of me and who I actually thought myself to be confused and frustrated me. On one hand, the adoration was highly flattering and ego seducing, but on the other, my mother had no interest or ability to see me as I was, which meant she was not paying attention, was not really listening to or looking at me at all. She despised any indications of weakness or self-doubt. She had no time or patience for my childlike ways.

Then there were my sisters, Anna, Beatrice, and Rose. They were fifteen, fourteen, and thirteen years old when I was born. I was their adored toy. I was their trophy.

I could not shake the ever-present feeling that I was a fake and would soon be found out. I could not just be a normal little boy with wild and playful instincts, daydreams and mischievous delight. I lived inside an impossible pressure and pretense to measure up to this person with superhuman qualities, when I was racked with uncertainty and confusion and very human needs.

My already emerging grandiosity alienated me from other children. They found me arrogant and conceited. I was not a bully so much as an unbearable snob. There was essentially no one good enough to be my friend. My parents confirmed this any time I brought home anyone to play with. They were highly critical and contemptuous. This was deeply embarrassing, so I eventually stopped bringing other children home.

I became progressively isolated. I had no one to talk to, no one to share my doubts with, no one to play with, and no real connection to anyone outside this mythic construction of my family. This created a very distorted vision of myself and the world. The only real contact I had was with my older brother, Milton, who was eleven years my senior. I shared a room with him for a period of time. He was a deeply unhappy fellow and seemed to direct his frustration and jealousy toward his knighted brother. He had great contempt for me and seemed to delight in sadistic pleasures, constantly inventing bizarre tortures and terrors; waking me by putting drops of alcohol in my eyes, hiding red ants in my underwear, convincing me something was terribly wrong with the shape and size of my genitals. He would lock me in the closet for hours, tie me to the bedposts until my wrists were raw. I lived in the great fear that he would one day harm me greatly or perhaps even kill me. His torture was conducted in secrecy. There was no one to turn to, as reporting him would have made me seem weak and unable to fend for myself. He knew this, of course, and unchecked, his perversity advanced in new and more frightening forms. I suffered silently, steeling and sealing myself, knowing there was no place for any expression of vulnerability or fear. I learned to separate from the shame and terror by constructing an alternative persona. I developed the capacity to feel nothing. I learned how to disappear.

I imagine it was at this point that I closed off the valves of empathy, for to feel anyone else's pain would have meant most surely to feel my own, and this was intolerable. The rage and terror I experienced on a daily basis were relieved through an obsessive fantasy life filled with visions of vengeance and destruction. My personality was molded on this fraught battleground. Deep in the center of me I became untouchable, and these endlessly played fantasies came to shape much of my later actions. No one would ever belittle, shame, or hurt me again. Not without the severest consequences. My isolation deepened as I grew into my teens, and that, with the onslaught of puberty, made me inordinately anxious, restless, and agitated. There was no place I could settle or relax inside or outside myself.

I was possessed by a demonic energy that I felt sure would lead me to violent crime, madness, or disaster. And perhaps I secretly wanted that, some crisis that would shatter and permanently eradicate this intolerable image, this absurd and overbearing idea of my superior perfection. It was through accidental fortune that on my seventeenth birthday, an uncle in show business offered to take me to my first moving picture. And it was there that a door opened and I found a way out of my misery. John Barrymore, Errol Flynn, Gary Cooper, Rudolph Valentino. Strikingly handsome, talented, but above all they were charming. Charming.

There on that huge screen I was introduced to the notion of charm. These men were able by their natural graces to please and seduce. They were able to hold their audience in rapt attention and fill them with deepest delight. Their control was effortless. It was as if they hypnotized their audiences simply by the inherent nature of their being. And it wasn't just their striking looks. I was quite a handsome young man and it had brought me no success. No, these men of the screen were somehow able to energize and use their looks with a divinely inspired charisma. It was as if their beauty had wit, as if it were elevated by an intangible intoxicating energy—an enigmatic dynamism that lured you in and kept you longing, kept you crazy, kept you hooked.

I went to the movies at every opportunity. I studied these men. I absorbed their every move, their smiles, their clothes, their confidence, their way of entering a room, their way of captivating women. I began to move as they moved, pose as they posed. I perfected the off-the-cuff sweep of the hand through my casually elegantly groomed hair, the penetrating but mysterious stare across the room. I suddenly had an image that was mine, not my mother's, an idea of who I wanted to be, and the image was all. I realized at that very young age that American culture was based on a picture, a fantasy. To succeed you needed to give yourself wholly to that creation.

Charm was my fortification. It served a dual purpose. It lured people in and it kept them excited and delighted long enough to come under my spell. Then, after, even when people felt demeaned or hurt or frightened by me, the charm confused them, but like a fly to honey, they clung to me in spite of their pain. My status among my peers transformed overnight from obscure to mysterious, from abhorred to imitated. I am not sure whether anyone, then or ever, really knew or liked me (and in full honesty what was there to like?), but they followed me, they were in awe of me; they wanted to be near me and have whatever I had.

Of course, it was shimmering illusion, a chimera, but who cared? Charm took the ugly off my grandiosity. It sweetened the arrogance. I was no less a snob, but now people admired me for it, as it seem justified. In those years before meeting your mother, I perfected my performance, and indeed it seemed my whole life was a grand act. Somehow this shining new rendition of myself seemed to ward off my father's harsh criticisms and contempt. He was impressed by my commitment to this new attitude, attire, and manner and suddenly had faith that I would indeed rise to be the golden boy he and my mother had dreamed of, bringing the family wealth and status. My sisters and mother became even more deeply enamored and devoted. I was the new American king, the pathway to a glamorous and glittering future for all. Even Milton, my vicious brother, was thrown off balance and seemed almost inspired by the entire effect. He gradually started to imitate my way of dressing and would sometimes accompany me to the movies.

The tortured and angry young man inside me was now firmly disguised, costumed in dashing handmade suits. He dressed in confidence and elegance and seemed, at least momentarily, to transform his enemies into admirers through style and charm. As you can imagine, this was a most synthetic remedy to what I can only identify now as soul sickness. I had been cast into the world as the exact opposite of the deep, reflective, philosophical man I had once dreamed of becoming. Instead I was becoming everything I secretly despised.

For I see now, after years of ceaseless self-obsession in the death realm, that there is no pain we can ever truly bury or avoid within ourselves. The tortured man I tried to leave behind would eventually surface. All the years of forcing him underground, all the sorrow and pain I ignored and did not care for, eventually metastasized into an entity and returned as a most terrifying fiend. He claimed my life then, and most regrettably, for the last thirty-one years he claimed my death in limbo. I realize I am speaking of him in the third person. I am by no means attempting to escape responsibility for his actions. It was more an indication of how profoundly detached I became from the person I shall call Shadow Man.

In the same way my parents had not seen or paid attention to the little boy I truly was, in the same way they idealized me and turned me into a king, I learned in turn to do the same thing to myself.

I became God in my own mind. I became all-powerful and perfect. Shadow Man had no place in that story. So I banished him the way I had been banished. If he was hurting, I became impatient with him and told him to snap out of it. If he was afraid or doubtful, I bullied him with merciless judgment. If the ragged edges of his low self-value surfaced, I dosed him with grandiose visions of my prowess and accomplishments. If he tried to remind me how far I had strayed from my spiritual longings, I shamed him into compliance by demeaning his impractical and nonsensical dreams and glorifying my rising fortune. I drank him away. I achieved him away. But all the while, Shadow Man plotted, seethed, and stewed. His sense of betrayal, his bitterness, his rage grew like volcanic lava bubbling beneath the surface of my skin. He would not emerge until much later. The ongoing friction caused by the growing disdain I had for myself combined with my arrogance and my utter inability and unwillingness to change my path assured a future in which I would become cruel and violent.

But Shadow Man would not emerge until much later. In those next years I built a life on charm, good looks, and snobbery. I moved in glamorous and fashionable crowds. I modeled for a time, and I was never seen in public without a bombshell actress or an elegant socialite on my arm. I was invited into the most exclusive clubs. I rose seemingly effortlessly to the top of society and the business world. The irony of course was that I despised those impostors and hypocrites who welcomed me and I had no interest in money. I found it beneath me and distasteful, merely a means to maintain my façade. But perhaps it was my very disdain for all of it that brought me fortune.

I've noticed that people often seem desperate for the person who has no interest in them. They gravitate toward the most critical and judgmental because that person confirms their deepest suspicion of being a worthless faker. I exploited this weakness to raise and sustain my position. People were intimidated by me, as they could sense my underlying contempt for their pathetic preoccupations. But my charm and looks distracted and drew them in. My life was a game to be mastered, a persona and an image to be styled and perfected. I was what was becoming known as a modern American man.

This is where your mother comes in. My playboy-bachelor days were beginning to sour—adorable rascal quickly descending into uncaring cad. I was close to fifty and had never had a relationship that lasted longer than a few months. I told myself and concerned others, particularly my older sisters, that I was holding out for "the one," but in truth, I dreaded everything about the notion of marriage and family. To be cooped up in a house with a boring woman and nasty children in dreary routine was a paralyzing notion.

It was about this time that I met your mother. I wish I could tell you we fell madly in love, but that is not what happened. (Although you must know I came to love your mother dearly in my way.)

Ours was a different situation. Your mother was twenty years my junior, and her beauty and youth made a striking contrast and complement to this graying, dashing older man. She was a knockout—blond, shapely, young, and gorgeous, a head turner. She had the poise of the beautiful and the passivity of the one beheld. But what drew us to each other is that we recognized ourselves in each other.

We were escape artists, both of us fleeing the prison of our stultifying pasts, the suffocation of our families, and various aspects of our uneven personalities. And we were self-made products—your mother, attempting to erase all signs of a poor, rural Midwestern upbringing, dyed her hair blond, changed her name, and fashioned a style and personality from studying divas in the movies. We were two solo performers who joined our strength in a crowd-pleasing duet, Arthur and Chris. We did everything but dance. So when people later made constant reference to us as Cary Grant and Doris Day, we knew we had arrived. We were pure invention, confection. We existed only in performance, and in those early years, our act was working.

We dined and traveled in New York City's most celebrated circles, our lives lubricated with very dry martinis. By then I had risen in the ranks of the ice cream company to a significant position. We dressed for our parts; we learned our lines and witty retorts. We had no idea who we were, and we most certainly knew nothing about each other. We didn't talk deeply when alone: our commitment was to a social rising concealed beneath a highly fashioned impenetrable veneer. We were curated mysteries, charming, evocative, with no entrance in.

For our first years, that worked fine for both of us. We had wealth and charm and looks and status and booze. Our sex was perfunctory, a performance too. Though perhaps that is more than you want to know. Our marriage was an equitable arrangement to elevate and sustain our position and power. A small business. I was the CEO and she my secretary. However, my grandiosity eventually got the better of me. How could I, with my superior character and wit, not continue such a legacy? How could I, with such charm and looks and intelligence, not reproduce? But if I'm honest, I don't think your mother and I thought of children as anything more than props for our evolving lifestyle.

From a young age I had always had a terrible feeling about having children. Some eerie sense that they would hurl me into unforeseen disaster. As an adult I had an allergy to them and they to me. Children were disturbingly foreign and terrifyingly familiar to me. On the surface they annoyed and irritated me, but the rub was much deeper. As it happened, having children was the catalyst for the return of Shadow Man. And I know now that my instinct not to have offspring was correct.

I had never been allowed to be a child. Children were undeniable evidence of who I had once been: vulnerable, needy, uncontrollable, messy, alive. They evoked unbearable absence in me, unbearable longing and feelings of deepest betrayal. They evoked a murderous rage. I despised their endless neediness because they dredged up my own.

But it was your birth, Evie, your arrival, that spun me into deepest bewilderment and distraction. Nothing had prepared me for the tenderness of you. Nothing had prepared me for the tenderness you would evoke in me. In your very early years I could not trust myself with you. Each time I held you in my arms, felt the soft flesh of your warm baby girl body, each time your little fingers wrapped tight around my grown man fingers, a surging pulse would rush through my whole body. The fire of this connection was a more compelling sensation than anything I had ever felt. More electrifying than winning the job of CEO, more erotic than orgasm, more ecstatic than deepest prayer. This energy filled every cell of my being. It called me out of myself.

No one had ever spoken of such feelings. I had no idea I would feel this way for my baby daughter. I did not know love. I had never been loved. I had been adored. I had been idolized. I had been savior. I had not tasted the honeyed milk of my mother's breast, nurturing and filling my soul and cells. My body had no way to receive or hold such sweet elation.

Each time I would venture toward your little body, I would find myself paralyzed, terrorized, filled with dread. Your mother found it comical and typical of men of my generation who were afraid of the foreignness and fragility of babies. But it was not that at all. How could I tell your mother that the touch of your new skin threw me into spasms of frenzy and fervor unlike anything I had ever experienced with her or any woman? That your tender essence had flung open the steel locker in my heart and loins and that I was possessed with an all-consuming desire that filled my days and nights with bliss and agony. How could I tell her that you were all I craved, that no other touch would ever be your touch, no sweetness would taste as sweet? I had betrayed her already.

You were my life force returned. You were the gift of passion made out of my own sperm and flesh. You were the calling, the invitation, the wild invocation of the sublime. I could and would not tell your mother anything of that. And so were planted the seeds of secrecy, the continuing manifestation of a dual life. I tried. I tried to stay away. In those early days, before I crossed the sea of the forbidden, I prayed to God to be relieved of this possession. My prayers were, in all honesty, half-hearted and insincere. Desire and destiny had already merged.

Shadow Man had been catalyzed by your birth, his rapacious hunger charged with the fury of a thousand wild horses rushing the winds of their freedom. His beastly sense of entitlement catalyzed inside the erotic essence of your tenderness. Your existence was somehow proof of his; your purity, your aliveness were the food he craved in order to feel his own. And he waited, patiently, like a lion in the bush ready for the right moment to seize his prey.

For your first years, I kept my distance. I hardly touched you, although at night I would often creep into your bedroom and stand by your crib as you slept. I would lean close and inhale the sweet scent of your baby breath. I would cover you in your little white blanket, and as I wrapped it around your tiny frame I would feel this sensation of falling, falling, tumbling into a milky universe that offered a safety and a delight I had never known. There in your crib-cum-altar, swaddled in white cotton, completely vulnerable and trusting, you were the radiant offering.

Then you turned five. There was something about five. Your face forming as my face, your brown eyes more fully alive and inviting, your infant body suddenly female, your cleverness revealed in your naughty sense of humor. You played with me. You teased me. You seemed somehow to know me as others had never known me, to delight in my ways, to find utter comfort in my embrace, to seek me. Unlike my mother, you had no image of who I was supposed to be. You loved me as I was. And I was the object of your pure, unmitigated adoration, the axis on which your being turned. What a powerful intoxicant! How was I to know that every daughter felt this way for her father? How was I to know that this adoration was a necessary stage in the development of the child and not to be corrupted? Instead it reaffirmed my grandiosity. Or rather, I used it to do as much. It removed doubts of my fraudulence. It filled my emptiness. A child had been born who perceived my godliness, who adored me the way my mother and my sisters had adored me, who worshipped as others should and would worship.

You were my treasure, my creation, now mirroring back my virtue and glory. And you were so much wiser than your few years. You seemed to intuit my needs and my moods. If I were in a melancholy state, which I often was, you would climb onto my lap and tap your little fingers on my cheek as if to distract me, as if to gently prod me out of my gloom. If I was angry, no one but you dared come near me. You would make faces at me, perform a clownish dance and make me laugh. You were the kindest little girl. Always helping others, overly sympathetic to those around you. There was never a time when someone cried that you didn't cry. Your heart was an angel heart. And you were mine. Daddy's little girl, my sweetie pie. That's what I called you. I see how this now makes you recoil. It didn't once. Sweetie pie. Sweetie pie. A tasty crust with delicious sweet warm fruit inside.

I did my best to contain and disguise my infatuation, but that kind of passion is impossible to mask. Your mother would constantly joke about how Evie was "the apple of her father's eye." And in some way, I think she was relieved and encouraged this attachment, as I had not come near you in your earlier years and she was worried I would never connect with you. All forces conspired to push us closer.

The tenderness. The tenderness shooting sweet sound waves over the border. Oh Jesus, such excruciating tenderness? It has been vanquished here in limbo. The empty nowhereness is most defined by the absence of beauty and kindheartedness.

Both were strictly outlawed from my boy beginnings, mistaken for fragility and unmanliness. These are surely what are most missing among the living. Do we fear anything more than tenderness? No war, no hate, no cruelty could make us feel so defenseless. What to do with it? Devour it, own it, crush it? It never occurred to me just to be with it, to be with you, to simply feel, appreciate, and share the depth of my affection. Instead, this startling affection became affliction, a burning curse. I was so empty and unprepared. Oh, Evie, I was so fond of you.

How did it begin? I know this is of great interest to you. How does one slip over the boundaries of what is permissible? How does one tear through a taboo coded in the essence of our collective DNA? The answer is slowly, gradually. I remind you I prided myself on being a very moral man. I was diligent with truth telling. I made no more money than we needed. I believed in moderation above all things. I trained all of my children in the strictest manners so you would always be generous and respectful of others. I prized my integrity.

Even in business, as the head of a corporation, I practiced fairness in all my interactions. I despised greed and waste and never cottoned to the nouveau riche who were vulgar and indulgent in their pursuit of wealth and possessions. You children had all you needed. Braces for your teeth, clothes and shoes. A yearly vacation, swimming and ballet lessons.

Oh dear, where am I going with this? I fear I'm slipping back, trying to persuade you of my goodness, and that is certainly not what you need or want. It's just to say that between who I became with you and who I thought myself to be—there was a great divide.

It began simply, easily embedded in the ordinary. We had a game. I would close my eyes and ask, "Where has my Evie gone? Why did she run away, where is she hiding?"

You would squeal with delight and shout, "I'm here, Daddy. I'm right here." My eyes still closed, I'd say, "Oh where oh where has my sweetie pie gone? Why does she not love me anymore?" You would pull at the leg of my pants, shake my thigh. "I'm here, Daddy. I'm right here." "Oh, I am so sad that she has run away. Why would she leave her daddy?" And you, shouting, would push at my arms and legs. "Open your eyes, Daddy. Open your eyes. I'm right here." Then the panic would set in. "Open your eyes, Daddy." You would climb onto my lap and your little fingers would do all they could to open my eyelids, but I would glue them shut. You would begin to cry, "Daddy, open your eyes. Open your eyes" and when I felt it had gone on too long, I would open my eyes with great surprise and delight. "Oh, there she is! There's my sweetie pie. But I am not sure she still loves her daddy!" And you, holding on to my face, looking into my eyes, would kiss me over and over on my cheeks and forehead. "I love you, Daddy, I love you, Daddy." "I don't know, Evie, I am not sure." And you would giggle and scream and punch me a little. "You are my daddy. All mine, Daddy." "I don't know. Are you sure, Evie?" And you would wrap your whole body around my body and rub your cheek against my cheek like some wild kitten in heat. I would hold you then and embrace you tight and lift you and spin you. "Yes, I think you do love your daddy. You do. You are your daddy's precious little girl." And you would laugh and shriek with relief and delight.

But then one day, I went too far and waited too long before I opened my eyes (I wonder now if I was pushing you to break) and you became desperate. "Daddy, Daddy, open your eyes. I'm right here." "I can't find you, Evie." You were screaming, crying, pulling back my eyelids with frantic fingers. "Open your eyes, Daddy, open your eyes! Look at me, look at me!" Then you began to plead and wail. "Daddy, open your eyes! Open your eyes!"

And I finally did, but by then you were inconsolable. You wailed and wailed as if you were experiencing some ancient and primal loss, as if you had tapped into the far-reaching sorrows of the universe. I tried everything to calm you down. I held you. I kissed you. I was stern with you and told you to stop. But you would not, or perhaps you could not.

And I don't know why it happened then. Perhaps I was shaken by experiencing the extremity of your attachment, the depth of your need for me. No one had ever before wailed for my attention. Perhaps it was your utter vulnerability and desperation that licensed him to finally take charge, but Shadow Man stepped in. And there and then he broke through the gate of sin. He began to pet your tiny body. First it was to calm. Or at least that's what he told himself. Hands slowly and soothingly across your chest, across the slight delight of budding nipples. This seemed to comfort and relax you some. But more it was for him. He wanted this. Down your soft stomach where you were tickled. Then slowly more methodically down, down to your cotton under-wear. I knew I should have stopped. I knew this was horribly wrong but I went on. I was a fifty-two-year-old man with a five-year-old child. My need, my desire more powerful than your comfort or sanity. Hand now touching but not touching the rising knob of your sweet spot. Imperceptible at first. Testing perhaps. I used your openness. I abused your trust. I told myself you wanted this. Your crying stopped. My touch was poisonous medicine.

I held you in my lap and all the boundaries melted away. Beyond taboo, beyond the law there was a galaxy of bliss, up and down, up and down. All of heaven seemed to cry out. Go on. Do not go on. Go on. This is against. This is your right. This is a crime. This is too much. Oh, Evie, I must stop.

I've gotten here too fast. It comes upon me now as it did then. I am sure it feels more like a reviving than a reckoning.

That day, Shadow Man crossed over and ended my life as I knew it. And yours. I traveled into a realm guided by nothing rational or familiar. I severed from the ship the mooring that defined me as a moral being and I was permanently cast out on a reckless, unforgiving sea. I can see this now, but back then the force that possessed me was so powerful and complete it overrode rational discernment.

You were an angel descended to save my soul and I yearned for salvation. You were the gift that would bring me to my heart when I hungered above all things to be human. In my distorted mind we married then, not as man and wife but deeper still, a covenant our bodies made with God and each other. You were mine, Evie. All mine. The special one. The one who had, through her beauty, innocence, and wits, moved me out of myself, taken me to heights I'd never known, broken through the constraints and made me a willing outlaw forever.

As Shadow Man saw it, the clandestine nature of our relationship deepened our connection, its preciousness and intimacy. Secrecy is a kind of drug, suffused with Eros, danger, and shared risk. It was our secret. No one could touch it or know it. It was our bond and promise. Shadow Man took full advantage. Our secret was a gilded box he could keep you in. Why would you tell? Why would you forfeit paradise?

You knew at five that you had won my heart, that I was yours, that there was no one else but you. A heady thing for any child, giving you an extraordinary and, I imagine, much distorted sense of power. You had only to bat your pretty eyes or gently lift and tease me with your sparkling crinoline petticoat and I was a goner. You taunted and flattered me, and then, when I was hooked, you would withdraw your attention, throwing me into a free-falling frenzy. I wouldn't be honest with you if I didn't tell you I relished it. Until that point no one had ever had this kind of power over me. No one had ever engaged with me, played with me, punctured the veneer. "Do with me, Evie, do with me as you will." And so it began—the days of ecstasy.

I would find myself in your room at some twilight hour. I only felt alive between the daylight and darkness in that crepuscular realm where dream and memory are indecipherable. That's how I controlled you. Those aphotic hours where others in the house were lost in sleep and you were in a trance, separated from your body. I would find myself sitting on your bed, somehow carried there by Shadow Man. You would pretend to be asleep. As if what was happening was not happening. You desperately wanted it and me to go away. I didn't go away. I never spoke, never uttered a sound. The silence was my power. Words would break the spell, make it real and ugly and what it was.

My hands, not hands, reaching up under your soft nightie and skin. You, Evie, your legs stretched out beneath the sheets were often stiff. I gently pulled your panties down. I would hold them to my face, inhale your life, inhale your damp. And you, your eyes still closed, praying it would stop. I would pry your legs apart for inspection, for me, your doctor. Your dirty doctor. First just exploring with my fingers to see what was needed. Gently investigating. Touching here touching there, touching light, touching more, to find the place that needed attention, that needed deepening.

I told myself this aroused you even though you were hardly breathing. I was your doctor and I was healing you. Of course you wanted me. *Touch it here. Touch it now, Daddy. Make it better, here.* I told myself I was doing this for you you you, for little Evie, slow and very light at first, almost not all, just grazing there, and I would touch it then and press and rub and move, move, then veer off slightly, the need to press and press and I would rub you then rub you back and forth and back and forth, rub and rub, your spot, our spot, rub, Doctor, stay with it, stay with it, do not stop, do your job, fix me there, bring it to life. Life, life. Oh God, Evie, you were life. Exploding there, small earthquake in my hand, shuddering ripping through the landscape. Oh Jesus. I feel ill and I am dead. How does a dead person vomit without a body?

I feel your revulsion and disgust. I see how this over-stimulation flooded your five-year-old body with agitation, dread and inexplicable grief. Pleasure became self-annihilation, sex became mourning. I did this.

Evie, what am I composed of now? What am I wrapped with beyond matter? Not skin as much as filaments of shame, not flesh as much as fibrous malintention. It will take time to unmask myself. Each layer gives way to another and each then seems most true. I hope you will be patient with me as I exhume these decomposing truths. I am terribly aware of the pain this is causing you. You have called for an autopsy of consciousness and it is slow going, chipping away at this psychic rigor mortis.

Let me continue this reckoning. There will be time to go back, time to filter it through another prism. For now, I will continue to share it the way I experienced it then, propelled without self-awareness, by an all-consuming selfishness and desire. And although I realize describing it as such may appear to get me off the hook or make you ill, this is how I experienced it then. I was not separate and aware of Shadow Man as I am now. I was inside him. My obsession with you erased all else. Everyone became invisible in your presence, everyone felt left out. Like trees planted in shadow, the family grew twisted and malformed in their hungry attempt to reach even a little bit of light. And their desperate reaching became an irritating burden.

Of course, somewhere I must have known my behavior was monstrous and revolting. But Shadow Man's righteous hunger overrode my guilt. He turned the tables and blamed the family for being needy and pathetic. He pushed them away as though they were clawing vermin. There was only one for him and that was you, Evie. And he had no willingness or ability to conceal it. The family grew to despise you for it. In that sense I set you up to be hated. And that would come to be part of what destroyed you. They couldn't blame me. I was the husband. I was the father. They needed me. So they blamed you. You were the reason they were deprived. You were the reason I was angry. You were the reason it all went wrong. You stole my heart. You banished them to darkness. Your name was Eve and you brought the fall onto the family. You were five.

And how could you ever feel right with yourself? You were a betrayer, a thief, selfish, too sexual, too strong, too all-consuming, stigmatized and condemned, cast forever out of their gloomy garden. Our gloaming nights continued. But Shadow Man was deeply wounded and voracious. With every transgression another hunger door opened inside him. With every unpunished trespass his boldness was empowered.

We lived in two worlds, you and I, Evie. The daytime and the night. But after time the line between them grew indistinguishable. My longing for you, my adoration, my obsession was too powerful and began to bleed over.

You had brought me back from the dead once before, awakened my heart and set my flesh on fire. Your sweet smell and touch and childlike energy pulsed through me like new blood. And like a vampire, I now needed it to live. I needed more. I needed to consume every inch of you, and this became violence.

Much to my chagrin, your mother arranged a vacation for her and me. I suspect she did this to get me out of the house away from you. It was an agonizing holiday on one of those dreary islands and I drank way too much. I couldn't bear that I had left you. I was unpleasant and unbearable.

When we returned, I opened the door and waited for you to run to me and rush into my arms as you always did. You were nowhere around. I found you upstairs playing with your brother. I entered the room. You hardly looked up. It was as if you didn't recognize me or had forgotten who I was. Your mother had to say, "Evie, don't you want to greet your father?" You walked over in a perfunctory way, sighed as if annoyed by the obligation to perform this rite, and barely kissed my cheek. Then you turned and without even the slightest smile or glance you went back to your game. My heart sank. *This isn't my girl. What has happened to make you like this?*

"Evie, you can do better than that for your daddy," I said trying to playfully engage you and conceal my panic and devastation.

"I'm busy now, Daddy."

Slap in face. Door shut. Heart ripped apart.

You are now competing with your mother. And how could you not? What a triangle I had created. What a psychic muddle. Your mother has become your adversary instead of your ally. I took my other wife away and you were heartbroken and abandoned. And instead of seeing how this might be an impossible thing to assimilate in your nine-year-old brain, I was beside myself, enraged by the rejection. How dare you withdraw your love from me when I am wholly devoted? How dare you think you have the power to cut me off when I am your father?

I never consider the pain you are in or how it must feel that I've left you for days to be with another. I never pause to think how utterly wrenching it must be that I made you believe you are the one, but only in secret and nobody knows. It was disgusting what I did. How tortured you must be, how agonizingly jealous. And years later, when you have compulsive serial affairs with married men, I know it is here that that pattern was imprinted. Here, where you came to see yourself as second, always and only number two. Never first to be married or taken. Never good enough to win the sole attention of any person's love. Only the whore they visited after dark.

But I did not think or feel any of this then. I was losing you. I was panicked. I could feel your suspicion emerging, a new hesitation and doubt. You were a sweetie pie, Evie, but also a fierce and defiant child. I could no longer trust you to remain faithful to me. I had to exert control, so Shadow Man took charge. I don't know if I can go further. I wonder if telling you what happens next is really doing you a service, Evie. Yes, I realize there is no apology without a meticulous accounting. But I seriously wonder if unearthing the depth of my cruelty and confirming it to you might be more devastating than curing. Will knowing the harsh specifics of my vicious actions serve your self-hatred, or your freeing?

At the time, everything had its own logic and trajectory and was fueled by my diabolical anger. You had betrayed me. You had pushed me to become like this. You were threatening to kill me by withdrawing your love. This was life or death. I had to do anything and everything to keep you in my power.

That night, Shadow Man came to your bed but his rules had changed. He was impatient and aggressive. He ripped back the sheets. He pulled your legs quickly and forcefully apart. He moved you roughly in the bed. He took what he wanted.

He no longer pretended to be a healer: he was a hunter; you, no longer a patient, but his prey. You were terrified. Your shock and judgment shamed Shadow Man and further provoked his fury.

This night was the dissolution of any pretense of parity. He was the boss. He would call the shots. You motioned for him to stop, tried to push him away, you were panicked and had clearly stopped breathing. Your eyes wide open seemed to be screaming.

His fingers, now hawkish talons, went further. They tore through your tightness. They ripped at tender flesh. They plucked off delicate feathers. They clawed and clawed at the golden gate of your precious garden, and when you refused entry, they forced their way in. You reeled from his depravity. You fought and fought and then you stopped fighting.

Shadow Man was ravaging the tenderness he craved the most. The tenderness that had made him helpless and exposed. The tenderness that had made him your prisoner. He would not be held hostage again. This was his territory and this his grand invasion.

Even as I touched your private places with my hands and force I was only sometimes aroused. I never put my penis inside you. I rarely got hard. I was oddly detached and uninvolved. And why am I telling you this, Evie? So you will think better of me? That I did not do the unimaginable? That I would not go so far?

Well, that is wholly disingenuous. I raped you, Evie. I raped you as a daddy doctor and I raped you now. I raped you with my seductive healing and I raped you with my rough fingers. I penetrated you again and again. Getting deeper and deeper into the place where you could be most hurt. Coercing you, forcing against your will. You were the country I was claiming. The land grab. The spoils of war. It didn't matter that I was despoiling the earth and all that grew there as long as I owned it, as long as it was mine. Better you be broken and bending. Easier to capture. Easier to control.

You had humiliated me by asserting your independence and autonomous thought, calling into question my behavior and loyalty. You had unmasked my selfish brutality and heartless cruelty and thus my true nature as a criminal and fraud. And you had threatened to withdraw your love. All these were high crimes in the Arthur Ensler court. Did I think my new tactics would win you back? Did I even believe that that was possible then? Or was it just plain ruthlessness and an exercise of brutal power? For what is rape but this? It is a grand mistake to confuse it with sex. It is a rage spasm, a violent overtaking, a desire to dominate and destroy. Like a heat-seeking missile it searches for the most vulnerable part of the victim's body in order to render the most damage. It is punishment, it is dominion. It is the eradication of the threat, the willing demolition of all the boundaries that make us human.

And it all felt necessary and preordained. It came like a groundswell from inside the depths of my body. It was ancient with its own trajectory and course. It was a fiery snake uncoiled, a confined stallion at the gates, now in full motion. It was inglorious and triumphant. And, like a nuclear cloud, terrifyingly awesome. Rape is the twisted refraction of all that has been denied and disallowed in men, unleashed at maximum velocity. What privilege looks like on a rampage. These savage nights went on too long. Shadow Man defied all danger, but the after-shocks were everywhere.

It began with night terrors. You would wake the house with terrifying screams, thrashing, babbling madness in your sleep. You mother would go to comfort you and you would push her away, shouting, "Get your hands off me. Let go. Get out. Don't touch me." Darkness and terror had seized you. You were haunted. These night terrors went on and on and seemed to get worse. You hardly slept. You lost your appetite. Your mother began to worry that something had possessed you, and of course it had. She wanted to take you to see someone but I insisted that we had a history of sleep disorders in my family. The signs of my ghastly pedophilia were beginning to bleed through.

Then the terrible infections started. Your mother would find you in the bathroom crying in the early hours. Burning, you said you were burning, and you would hold yourself between your legs and rock and whimper and rock and cry. Nothing could soothe you. You were hysterical. At least three times your mother took you to the doctor. Chronic urinary tract infection was the diagnosis. But no one could explain how they had started. "What has happened to our girl, Arthur? How could all of this have come over her at once?" I could smell her suspicion. And at the same time as I was nearing being caught, it was clear some force had seized you and was taking you in a very bad direction. Your demeanor changed. You were suddenly sullen and unresponsive. No longer carefree, chatty, and inquisitive, you became depressed and withdrawn.

You moved like a ghost. You rarely lifted your head and hardly spoke. You never washed your hair and it was always stringy and dirty. You were unable to concentrate in school and did poorly in class. You could not pass an exam. You seemed unable to remember or contain anything at all. You were becoming stupid. You were demoted to the lower ranks and lost your closest friends. Other children could smell your desperation and avoided you like the plague or teased and taunted you. I despised you for this weakness. But how could I admit that I was responsible for your decline? How could I tolerate the visible outcome of my brutality? Instead I humiliated you further and made you feel your badness had made this happen. That my sweetie pie had, through her assertion and rejection, become a dirty shameful girl.

It was around this time that we were called in to your school one day. You were around ten. We found you in the principal's office, your eyes swollen from crying, your little dress muddy and a mess. Two boys had chased you from school at the end of the day and there, in the center of the square, had thrown you to the ground and pulled your panties down in front of hundreds of onlooking children. You were inconsolable, whimpering and pathetic.

I was furious and blamed you. I told you to stop your crying. How could you provoke this and let this happen? What slutty thing had you done to make them do this to you? I imagined you were playing them as you had played me. The tables were turning. I never asked you to explain what happened. I did not comfort you or take your side.

That night I came to your bed. Did I imagine I would undo all this with just a gentle corrective? Did I truly believe that with a few comforting words and a soothing touch you would suddenly change back? Talk about magical thinking! I had smashed this delicate china cup into a million pieces and no amount of sweetness or charm would make it whole again. Immediately upon entering the room I could feel a poisonous energy. You were turned away on your side, seemingly glued to the wall. Shadow Man touched you and tried to turn you over, but you were cold, rigid as a corpse. Even Shadow Man stopped. He shook you and prodded you like a panicked dog with an unresponsive master, whispering, "Turn around, Evie, turn around. Wake up. Look at me." You remained frozen. No breath, no movement, no warmth coming from your little body. It was as if you had left yourself and gone looking for another family somewhere else. As if you had left me and were never coming back. "Evie, wake up, turn around, come back. I'm here." Not a breath, not a movement, not a sound. Had you actually died or were you like a possum protecting yourself from a predator, willing yourself into a state of thanatosis?

I felt a sickening dread. I had done it. I had killed you, murdered the soul of the being I most adored, the one who had given me life. I had violated her body, betrayed her trust, I had ripped the burning wick out of the brightest candle. I wanted to get on my knees and howl and beg forgiveness. I began to shake you and shake you as if to bring you back. "Wake up, Evie, wake up." Your body remained rigid and stiff as I rolled you over. I shook you harder and harder.

And then you opened your eyes. You did not blink or look in my direction. Instead your eyes were staring off, far off into another universe. A world that would hold your deepest secrets. A world that would house your wounded heart. A world I would never be invited into. I had lost you. Soul murderer.

Shadow Man was many things but not a necrophiliac. This was the last time he visited your room at night. You had willed yourself dead so he could take no more life. But that didn't mean he wasn't angry and vengeful. Several days after, you cut off your hair. You furiously chopped it into hideous mess. After that you refused to wear dresses. You dressed only as a boy. Overnight your personality changed. You became defiant and obstinate. Your answer to every question was an insolent *No*. You never smiled. You demanded that the family call you Eve and refused to answer to Evie, my moniker of endearment. You never asked for help or expressed any needs. You let no one in.

Your pretty face lost its pretty. Your lips pursed, your cheeks and forehead tensed in a permanent scowl. You slumped and refused to stand up straight. Your table manners were disgusting. Your once sparkling brown eyes were now a muddy river of self-pity and sorrow. Your hair, what was left of it, lost its shine. You were quickly becoming a flat, disturbing, embarrassing child.

And I despised you for it—my murder victim tormenting me by residing in my house, forcing me to witness every day the decomposition and rot of her young being. Forcing me to face the consequences of my despicable actions. It was intolerable. It was madness. Where had my Evie gone? My sweetie pie? But of course I knew the answer. Her trust, her force of light, her goodness, her beauty were too much for me and so I violated, invaded, smashed and disfigured them and her. Then, after she had become this bitter damaged creature, I was disgusted and blamed her. I withdrew my love. Yes, I withdrew my love from you. I never gave it back. I lived to hurt you after that. To hurt you for your unconcealable hurt. Thus began the reign of punishment, violence, and terror.

I vividly remember the night it began. You were standing in the den and you had just turned ten. You were slouched and had on a dirty T-shirt that I had asked you repeatedly not to wear. You were asking if you could spend the night at your girlfriend Judy's house. You were manipulatively sweet, hoping this honey-coated plea would conceal your desperation. I said no. I said it right away. I don't know why. Perhaps it was because I knew it was something you wanted so frantically. Perhaps because you were daring to manifest your autonomy. Perhaps because there was nothing about you I liked anymore and I wasn't about to reward you with anything.

You frowned and made a terrible face. You didn't like my answer. I told you, "Smile when I tell you something, smile when I give you my answer." You didn't smile. You went on, "Why? Judy only lives up the street, I don't have school. We made a plan." Impertinent child. How dare you question my authority. "It isn't fair, Daddy. What is the reason?" "I told you no, Eve. That is reason enough.

I don't need to give you an explanation," and once again, I told you to smile. You didn't smile. You stared at me with contempt. "I'll give you one more chance." My rage was boiling, my face on fire. And you waited as long as you possibly could, pushing and daring me to cross that edge. Then you turned your face into the most disrespectful smirk, a disdainful smile refusing and mocking my command.

And Shadow Man instantaneously leapt up and with all his might he smashed his hand across your insubordinate face. Your whole body went flying across the room until it crashed against the wall and you dropped like a flimsy rag doll to the floor on top of carpet fuzz and crumbs. And through your tears and shock, you smiled the sickest smile. You smiled and smiled as if you were some deranged robot doll. You wouldn't stop smiling. You were no longer there. It was as if Evie had been displaced and this new Eve, emboldened ghost, was now in charge. Shadow Man versus Shadow Eve. War had been declared.

Your mother was speechless but oddly did not intervene. I think secretly she had been waiting and longing for this moment when the spell would be broken and I would denounce you and return to her. The whole family let out a collective sigh. They had a front row seat for this dramatic and brutal scene in which my obsessive adoration and all-consuming devotion to little Evie were publicly murdered.

And having been deprived and ignored for so many years, the family was more than happy to join my noble army. Eve was the enemy now. Not their husband and father. They wholeheartedly aligned themselves with me, arming me with information for my daily punishments and securing your permanent banishment. You were cast out of paradise that day. You, once held highest, were tossed from the roof to live outside alone in dirt. You, once the center of my melting heart, were banished into purgatory.

And telling you this, I am filled with horror and regret, feeling for the first time how you must have felt. The shock. The disbelief. The utter loneliness. To be exiled, to have been made to believe you were everything and then in one violent blow erased to nothing. How could you, at ten years old, possibly handle this? Who could you turn to for help when I had turned all against you? How could you not go mad when you were now taken to be the carrier of all that was deceitful and bad? Scapegoated and stigmatized, you became, in that moment, fall girl for your father's sins. I see you wince. I warned you this would not be easy.

If it's any consolation, the murdering of my fondness for you essentially murdered me. All that was bitter and hateful metastasized in me. I became depressed and chronically disappointed. I drank uncontrollably. As I grew into my sixties my charm dimmed. My impatience, arrogance, and intolerance shrank our circle. We were more and more isolated, and although your mother had me back, she was delivered a monster.

I realize that how my actions affected me is not your concern (may be painfully reminiscent of my telling you after each beating that it hurt me more than it hurt you), but I wanted you to know there was some justice. For if I have learned anything here in this torturous realm, it's that there is no hurt we consciously inflict on another that does not come back tenfold.

I was well practiced and knowledgeable in the art of breaking people. Hadn't I from early childhood been broken, severed from myself, forced into a grandiose and impossible persona? Hadn't my parents, in pursuit of their Divine King, killed off any semblance of my vulnerability, empathy, humility, humanity, or doubt? Hadn't they taught me through strictest Germanic child-rearing techniques that the job of the parent was to remove all willfulness and wickedness in the child through scolding and the rod? That disobedience constituted a war against the parent and any obstinacy must be met by blows?

The tracks of that training were deeply instilled in me, and the harrowing years with my brother Milton had provided me with additional tools for inflicting torment. I see this now. I was not conscious of any of this then. And it was in fact the denial of the violence and cruelty I had endured from my parents and Milton that allowed me to perpetrate deeper, more devastating violence on you. And there was an adjoining, pressing mission—to keep you submissive and quiet so you would never expose our secret. I became a righteous torturer.

I worked daily to destroy your character and break your will. I devised fault, failure, and mistakes in you. I became brilliant at it, always sussing out your weaknesses and moving in. For example, I knew you were a deeply ethical child. You shared everything even when you wanted it desperately for yourself. You had an implicit and demanding sense of loyalty. You never told on your brother or sister, not even if it would benefit you. I could never get you to turn on the others. I knew how important it was for you to be good. I knew that in some way your life depended on it. So I made you wrong and bad. This was to destabilize you. Then I would remain in charge. Then I would maintain control over the family narrative, and I did until the end.

I made you believe things about yourself that were never true. First and foremost, I made you believe you were a liar. The irony was that you were a scrupulously honest child. But the threat of my ongoing terror and brutalization made it impossible for you to tell the truth to me, and each time you lied, it was proof and ammunition. And why was that honesty so important to me? Why was it my ongoing obsession? The answer is obvious now, after years of endless churning. When your own being is controlled by a lie, apply the tactics learned in the school of power and duplicity. Turn the tables. Make the victim of your lie the liar.

Commit wholeheartedly to this, embellish the story constantly, repeat the narrative faithfully and consistently so that you and everyone around you eventually forget the original lie and certainly lose the compulsion, will, or courage to pursue the truth. Isn't this the story of so much of history? The powerful create the lie, package it, and propel it on its way for all eternity.

Of course, the repetition of the lie alone will not be enough to solidify the narrative or secure its permanence. This is a much more extensive project. The whole environment surrounding the lie must be altered as well. You must work to break the community (who consciously or unconsciously know the truth) of their capacity to believe themselves or each other. You must enact a scheme that will steadily and assuredly convince them of their own stupidity and lack of credibility. I devoted a great deal of energy and time to this endeavor. And one of the most chilling aspects of it was to discover that in convincing you and your mother of your stupidity, I actually made you stupid. This of course only made me despise you more.

Credibility is at once an amorphous and a specific thing. It's suffused with intangible qualities: sureness, confidence, calm. Those who have been beaten down and been made to feel like worthless idiots can never exude such assurance and poise. They appear desperate because they are desperate. No one has ever believed them, and so they are compelled to resort to extreme measures: emotionality, hyperbole, exaggeration. They speak louder, they wave their hands. They appear hysterical. Eve, you started to embellish facts and exaggerate. You would tell me, "Daddy, I want to drive to school. Everyone in my class is driving a car."

And I would say, "Everyone, Eve? Every single person?" And you would say, "Yes, yes, yes, everyone," and I would say, "Okay then, go gather their names, bring them to me. Show me the everyone." At which point your face would fall. Case closed. Guilty as charged.

It's a vicious circle, really, and one that I exploited. You refuse to believe the person. They become extreme in order to prove their case. Their exaggeration and over-statement erase their credibility and eventually, over time, they too begin to doubt themselves as well as everyone who witnesses this ongoing enactment. The whole family came to mock you, Eve, and your huge pronouncements based on little to no facts, your almost fanciful exaggerations of almost everything, your extreme displays of emotion in delivering these absurdi-ties. And so the project fulfilled itself and you became the one who could not be trusted, the one no one believed.

I can see now how this robbed you of sureness of your own seriousness and intelligence. I know you have been plagued with an agonizing and debilitating belief that you are stupid in the face of others who have not had to resort to such hyperbole in order to be seen or believed. It was trickier with your mother. I had to make her seem stupid but not too stupid, otherwise the legitimacy of her allegiance to my authority would have come into question.

My attacks on her intelligence were more nuanced and less frequent and had to be moderated with care, undermining her enough to assure complete dominance and her total dependence, but not so extremely as to make it seem as though her choices were not her own.

I know you are wondering, was all this a conscious maneuvering on my part? Did I methodically manipulate and design this wickedness? And the answer is not clear. I will not lie here, Eve, I had come to despise you. You had taken life away from me. You had opened my heart and made it dependent on fresh blood and then you had cut it off at the arteries. I was a drowning privileged man. Did I know then that what I was doing was diabolical? Did I have an inner moral sense that what I did was terribly off? Perhaps, but even in my worst rages, my most violent attacks, when I flashed on your bloody face or the welts on your legs or the terror in your eyes, even if there may have been a passing flinch, the justification for my actions always subsumed my guilt or self-doubt.

I can tell you I had anxiety. I had rage. I had melancholy. It is why I drank so much. At the time I attributed it more to existential despair, and to the pressures of running a company, but it has occurred to me as I have been spinning in limbo that perhaps there was some place deep inside me that felt horrified by my actions as I felt horrified by my own father and brother. How much self-awareness does a life of privilege and entitlement afford the entitled? If you are birthed into a particular paradigm that serves you, what would compel you to look outside?

You may argue that others who have had such indoctrination found the motivation to revolt. Their inner compass signaled they were headed in the wrong direction and they changed course. I never met such men. It seems to me that change is usually catalyzed by some deprivation or catastrophe—some event or series of events that forces one into crisis and collapse. No man I knew would ever openly question himself in front of others. He would never admit defeat or doubt. And as I told you, my sense of entitlement was steely and impenetrable. My exaggerated sense of self-importance repelled all incoming objects. It simply never occurred to me that anything I ever felt compelled to do could possibly be wrong.

And because, as a child, I had been filled with exaltation rather than comfort, my narcissism triumphed over my ability to care.

Was I a coldhearted monster, or a man with a broken and revengeful heart? Is there a difference? Does it matter? Certainly not in terms of the pain my cruelty inflicted on you. Was I consciously aware of Shadow Man? Wasn't I a witness to his brutality? Couldn't I have stopped him? Was I a psychopath? That would be an easy out.

No. I was not insane. I was a privileged, forceful man. I lived above this world, above criticism, above reproach. I was programmed to control, to win at all costs. You were my child. You were my property. You would do as I instructed you to do. When you didn't, it was my duty to enact the discipline and punishment that would bring you around. This is how I had been raised. I was doing what was done to me. I was doing as I was taught. But there is another, far more wicked truth. As Shadow Man had drawn me over the borders of sin when you were five, he was now hauling me into hell. Sure, it was my upbringing that favored these specific tools of punishment, but it was a much more terrifying thing. It is almost impossible to confess. But at this moment, I am bizarrely possessed by a poem by T. S. Eliot. A poem I once and often recited to you about cats. It is ringing through my head, blocking out all else.

The Naming of Cats is a difficult matter,
It isn't just one of your holiday games;

You may think at first I'm as mad as a hatter
When I tell you, a cat must have THREE DIFFERENT
* NAMES.*

This poem may seem like an incongruous departure, but it is not. You were sixteen. You had a cat. You loved her dearly. She was a bit eccentric, but she made you very happy. I was indifferent to animals, but through your vast and creative appreciation, I came to see the wonder and whimsy of this gray-and-white-striped tiger. Her name was strange. I believe it was Backhand. And somehow in the midst of this war between us, this quirky cat invited surprising and delightful expressions of myself. At night, when Backhand would go into heat, we would listen to her agonizing moans echo throughout the woods and we would howl with embarrassment and delight. When you were not around I would sneak into the kitchen where I never went and feed her salty herring. I would whisper to her and she would rub me and follow me room to room. I was unable to conceal how deeply this pleased me. And you would be shocked to come home sometimes and find her curled up, purring in my lap.

Everyone took joy in my love of the cat, as they had never seen me playful or gentle except with you. I know how much it meant to you that I had come to cherish this furry being you loved so dearly. Backhand became the repository of our tenderness, the remnants and reminder of what lived between us but could no longer be expressed. This soft and pulsing creature, manifestation of our loss and our yearning.

Then the unthinkable happened. You were away for the afternoon with friends. I was in the house when we heard the sound of tires screeching and then a small commotion outside the house. Your mother and I ran out and there to our horror was Backhand's listless body lying in the middle of the road. I was beside myself. I ran to her and without even thinking, picked her up. She was bloody and broken but still seemed to be breathing. It was at this moment that you drove up. You jumped out of the car and ran to see what was going on and when you saw Backhand draped and looking lifeless in my arms, you let out a piercing scream. An unbearable shriek that tore through the impenetrable walls of my defenses. I found myself crying. Tears sliding down my cheeks. Tears of sorrow for the fragile life in my arms who was crushed. Tears for all the ways I let you down. Tears of loss and regret for my carelessness, for this singular and remarkable gift of you, which I had not protected but instead destroyed. Tears that matched your aching grief for yet another comfort that had been taken from you. Tears for this cat, your companion, your cozy friend, shattered, smashed, and close to death.

And you saw my tears. I could not hide them from you. And this made you cry even more, but for that moment you were not alone. I was crying with you. I felt your pain and it was mine. For maybe the first and only time, a window opened into the pulpy business of my tortured heart. You found yourself there, Eve. And although this window never opened again, it was undeniable evidence of another story. I know it stayed with you.

Backhand did not die. Her bladder was injured but she learned to pee again. Her jaw was broken and was wired into a new configuration. Her once adorable and open face was twisted and disfigured. Even her smile became a grimace. Just like my Eve, violence had made its mark on all her features. And just like my fierce and unstoppable daughter, she had nine lives. Her will to survive surpassed her reliance on beauty. Why does this event come to me now at the most grueling hour of my accounting and confession? It must seem like a bizarre departure and distraction.

This letter has not been easy. Each confession demands a rigor and precision, each unmasks a more onerous intention. Each forces me to use flaccid, unexercised muscles of moral self-scrutiny. Each stretches me beyond my mental capacity. My life was wholly devoid of self-awareness. I had no motivation or interest in examining my reasons or behavior. And of all the things I feel most ashamed, it is this arrogance, this superiority and pride. And yet it has become so much my nature that I cannot imagine how to be without it.

Without it, how could I possibly be a man? My lord, to be dead and still worrying about being a man! Even in limbo I feel compelled to prove myself and no one is here. Proving myself to God perhaps. Showing him I will not be defeated. That even in the face of eternal torture I will not surrender this conceit.

You are asking me to question the very nature of what it means to be a man. And even to submit to the exercise assumes a defeat.

The irony, of course, is that I've already lost. But the mind is a seductive labyrinth camouflaging a cage. And ironically, I am caught believing that if I surrender my privilege I will disintegrate, even as I'm already a nonentity.

I was brought up in a time when men were praised for controlling and withholding their emotions. They were admired for their steely steadfastness and knowing the way. They never apologized. They never asked questions. They never explained. They never revealed their hand. They didn't speak. Their silence was evidence of their strength and virility. They were expected to master the world and to lead with determination and assurance. The thrust of a man's existence was to maintain his position.

And even in death, absent of body and no apparent self, as absurd as it may sound, there is part of me that would rather face an eternity in torturous limbo than relinquish this identity.

For what other framework do I have for the explanation of my being? What other demarcation renders me value or meaning?

It has become increasingly apparent, writing this letter to you, that this structure of identity has been the cause of great harm to you and others and is most definitely the reason I am suspended in torturous spinning. I see now that this particular notion of manhood is highly questionable, as great violence is always required to preserve it. And it seems to me that any structure predicated on the need to destroy another is not just or sustainable. But as much as I can grasp this analytically, giving it up is a whole other matter. It feels nothing short of asking one to delete one's ego. For this patriarchal blueprint has been implanted into the basic psychological compendium: ego, superego, id, man.

Perhaps the only way to dissolution is what you have called me to do: probe the exact nature of the harms inflicted, do my best to open myself to how my behavior affected you, and trust that the alchemy of this exercise will allow me to be more and more honest in the service of your freedom. So, I have avoided this last testimony long enough. It feels treacherous and searing to put to print. It cannot be taken back. And the quandary that underlies it has gnawed and pursued me like a demon and given me no rest. Did I, in your teenage years, set out to kill you? Did I do it with conscious intent? This much I know: there was more than one incident in which I could have taken your life. After the first terrifying encounter, I did not desist. With each new dispute, I became more volatile. I knew alcohol was fuel for Shadow Man and I did not stop drinking. My fear for your safety was never an inhibiting factor. In fact, I blamed you each time for provoking me and truly believed it was you who were responsible for my behavior.

Breathe, Arthur, breathe. May the gods take me to hell!

I wanted you dead, Eve. I tried on several occasions to murder you. I had to kill what I had already destroyed.

I had to erase the evidence. And you, being deeply intuitive, felt this filicidal thrust. But in order to keep your sanity you had to deny it. For how could you live knowing your own father was conspiring, consciously or not, to kill you? And this act of denial created a pattern in which you would later be constantly blinded and drawn to the most violent and wounding. You would put yourself in serious danger throughout your life, time and time again, because you could not read it as such and because it was so familiar. You would seek out hurtful people and situations in hopes that you would one day be strong enough to conquer them. And most scarily, eventually your sexual pleasure would come to be laced with this danger.

I made a masochist of you.

And I believe what got identified in you as suicidal in your early teens may have in fact been you wanting to finally be murdered and relieved of the ongoing terror and dread. There are incidents that haunt me. I share the details of each with the hopes that a specific and arduous accounting confirms your memory. I share them to make transparent the depth of my ferocity and brutality. I share them so I may bring to light my unending project of terror and torture. I am responsible, Eve. I was this wicked. I was a coward of this highest order.

I beat a child half my size. I battered a little girl. I used my hands, my fist, and belts as whips. I interrogated you mercilessly. I called you every terrible name. I insulted every fiber of your being and body. My intention was to humiliate and extinguish. My tactics knew no bounds. And then I further stultified and negated you by threatening you if you dared to scream or beg or cry. I denied you an outlet for your anguish or terror or pain. It gave me satisfaction that this agony would fester and lodge in you. It's how I made my mark. How I burrowed in and left my poison.

Horrifying incidents replaying over and over on one punishing, unrelenting loop for fifteen years here. Pieces of events, objects, fragments, flashes like those early movies, which cut rapidly scene to scene.

. .

Pizza parlor. Classless joint. Family dinner. No martinis. Annoyed. You antsy in your seat. You're reaching for things. Sit up straight, Eve. Sit still. I say something. You immediately disagree. Stupid, girl. "No, I'm not. I'm right." Boom.

Fist lands in the center of your stupid face. Blood spurting from your nose. Crimson stains on red-and-white-checkered tablecloth. You frozen, staring with contempt, blood streaming down your face. The family is horrified.

"Chris, get her out of here. Clean her up." Your mother trying to move you quickly through the restaurant. You stopping. Displaying your face for entire room. Embarrassing me. Disgracing the family.

Outside I grab your arm hard. Drag you through the parking lot. I throw you in car. Whimpering in back seat. "Shut your mouth, Eve. Shut your dirty stupid jackass mouth."

• •

Shaken awake out of deep sleep. Your mother rattled and alarmed. Get up, Arthur. Get up. Eve smoking in her bed. Storming your room.

You outside your window on the roof half naked with a cigarette. Whore. Slut. Grab you. Pull you roughly through the window. Beat you. Smash you. Drag you down the stairs.

Throw you outside. In the dark, in the cold, in your underwear. Now you'll live as a whore on the front lawn for all the world to see. Slammed, locked the door. Left you there.

• •

Get down here, Eve. Get down here now. Stand there. Against the wall. When I speak to you, look at me. Look at me. Where did you go Thursday night? You mumbling under your breath. I can't hear you, Eve, speak up. Where did you go? Who were you with? Who were you with, Eve? Didn't you tell me you were staying after school? And you did not. Did you lie to me? Did you lie? Lie. How dare you lie to me? Dirty liar! Hands around your lying head. Hands smashing head against the new wood-paneled wall. Banging. Banging head. Concrete ball. Want to smash it to pieces and watch all the stupid lies fall out. Bang bang. Smash head.

"Chris, Chris. This child is rotten to the core. Go, go and get a knife from the kitchen." Your mother doesn't move. Get the goddamn knife. Your mother leaves the room. She doesn't return.

. .

Hands around your neck choking you. I cannot stop. Choking and choking. You cannot breathe. Your face is red. Gagging. Your mother screaming, "Stop. Stop. She cannot breathe." Choking more. You turning blue.

Something in me doesn't want to stop. Something in me wants to choke the stupid life out of you. Choking and choking. You're no longer breathing. Your mother pulls me off.

· ·

I catch you sneaking and whispering on the phone. No phone calls allowed. "Hang up this phone, Eve. Get up here now."

"Get my belt, Chris. Get my belt." She hesitates. "Get it now!"

I wrap the end around my hand. Bend over the bed, Eve. Bend over now. Whip and whip your legs. I can see welts already forming.

You will not go back to school. You will not be a cheer-leader. We are sending you to reform school and you will sleep in the basement from now on with the dog. I drag you down the stairs and push you into the cellar. In the morning you are gone. You don't come back for weeks. I won't allow your mother to call and find you. We don't call school. We never ask around.

One day you suddenly appear. I've instructed the family to act as if you've died. No one is allowed to acknowledge or speak to you or they will be punished. You are driven mad. You leave again.

. .

I am reeling now imagining the tsunami of fright you were pushing back in your little body and being since you were five. How this daily and extraordinary exertion taxed and tore your muscles and blew out the fragilely webbed fibers of your nervous system. Your violent death was ever present. And each murderous episode escalated the stakes and the brutality.

I imagine it was all you could possibly think about. When would I strike again, how would you protect yourself? Would you die? You lived in constant anxiety and dread, and these emotions eventually became the neurotic ingredients of your character. (I am sure it's why you later drank and did drugs, trying to soothe yourself.) This high-level stress made it impossible for you to think or study or play or dream or learn or concentrate or remember anything. You could not relax. You did not sleep.

Then there were the ongoing, more methodical terror punishments. I needed to find ways to constantly keep you on the hook. These involved bizarre and creative castigations, concoctions of humiliation, brutality, and pain. One particularly stands out. I will call it the Ping-Pong Paddle Sessions. I have my secretary, Annette, type up an accounting each week on my office stationery. From the Desk of Arthur S. Ensler. A list of each bad thing you have done, each lie, each transgression. I gather details from many sources and undercover scouts in the family. Each week I call you into my bedroom. I make you read the list out loud. Then I ask you to count the number of your wrongdoings. Sometimes it's six. Sometimes it's ten. It's never fewer than four. I ask you if you have anything to say to me. You mumble, "I'm sorry." "I can't hear you, Eve, do not mumble." And then you say too loudly. "I'm sorry." Then I ask you one more time, and finally you say it sincerely, obediently, and politely, "I am sorry, Daddy." I say. "Better." "Now go and get the Ping-Pong paddle." You know where it is kept and you know its purpose. For each item on the list you will get a hardy whack.

I tell you take down your jeans and underwear. You do this hesitantly. "Speed it up. I don't have all day." I tell you lie facedown over the bed. You know the drill. You lay there, your bare and tender rear end exposed so vulnerably on my bed. You are sixteen. You are already a woman. I can see your hands already clutching the bed covers. The Ping-Pong paddle has a ridged green rubber covering and when I smack it hard enough it leaves indentations. This is my goal. Tattoo the design of punishment so you will not forget. The first paddle you are brave but after two you try to protect yourself with your hands. I tell you move your hands away. You begin to cry. "Please, Daddy. Stop. I didn't mean it. Please, it hurts. I'll do better next time." "Move your hands. Don't you cry." I smack. I whack. I smack. I whack until I'm done. When it's over you stand and pull up your underwear and pants. Your body is trembling. You are crying. I can see it isn't easy for you to walk. You limp out. This goes on week after week. This is our ritual. You pull down your underwear, bend over the bed. I lift my paddle.

Then one day your attitude has changed. You come and read the list with energy. You do not pause but say with almost hypersincerity, "I am sorry, Daddy." You go right away and get the paddle. You confidently take down your pants and underwear. You do not clutch the bed covers. You do not scream or beg or cry. I smack you seven times. When it's over you stand up. You pull up your pants and underwear. You look me in the eye and smile the broadest smile. "Thank you, Daddy. That felt so good. I loved it. I look forward to doing it again." And you all but skip out of the room. You won, Eve. The Ping-Pong Paddle Sessions stopped right there and then. You won this battle, but at what cost? Who and what had you become? What new entity had my malevolence constructed?

Where did your rage and hurt and suffering go? You seemed to bury them under this new hardened and numb persona. But unlike Shadow Man, who would exact revenge and wrath upon the world, you would eventually turn it entirely on yourself. This once highly penetrable, feeling creature could no longer be accessed or found. You could not be touched. Your windows shut. It began that night when Shadow Man found you in your room appearing dead, but now it consumed your personality.

And you easily could have become a very dangerous person. Perhaps it was the magnitude of your heart or simply being a powerless girl, but instead this began the years when you consciously or not set out to destroy yourself. I no longer had to lift a hand or raise my voice. You were more violent to yourself than my worst imaginings. And here it can only be said, with deepest despair, that I had, through my brutality, turned this angel tender girl who cherished life into a madly suicidal teenager. I watched with horror, disgust, and remorse as you went on a reckless rampage. It lasted years. You smoked and drank incessantly. You were stoned or high throughout most of your days at school. I believe you were stealing.

You hung out with nefarious characters, drug addicts, dealers, and criminals. You were having sex with these miscreants who were often three times your age. It was only a matter of time before you got pregnant.

You became a wild hippie. You stopped wearing a bra, grew armpit hair, and looked a disgrace. Everything you did was a slap in my face. And I knew violence was no longer a deterrent. Even when I grounded you and refused to let you out of the house, you would defy me by sneaking out in the middle of the night. You were reckless in the car. You were willing yourself to crash, to be caught, to be arrested, to be obliterated. Your grades and performance in school were assuring you would not go to college or have any future. You stopped eating and were frighteningly thin. You were hyper and you never stopped moving your leg. You were intolerant and disagreeable. There was nothing that could pull you back in.

At eighteen you were in a madly spinning downward spiral, on your way to some irreversible tragedy or possibly death. I blamed this on your willfulness and badness. I blamed and shamed and hurt you more. I never for one moment tried to prevent you from falling.

What is this gnawing, burning sensation in my chest? Oh Eve, oh Eve, is this your heart inside me? Am I feeling what you were feeling then? This is too much. Oh anxiety, oh loneliness, oh despair. Despair.

The sinking impossibility of a life, the hatred of yourself, the suffocating rage at me, at your mother, at your family, at the heartless world that brought you here. Paralyzing dread. No place to turn to. No one understands. Claustrophobic cage of hopelessness closing in. *Let me out. Let me out of here, out of here.* How did you breathe, Eve? How did you survive?

What is happening? The vapid nothingness of limbo suddenly growing dim, growing dark. A falling night. But not night so much—more like a ruinous pit. I must be tumbling into hell. Demonic cave-blackened wound. Contractions of shame cut through me. Dying a thousand deaths but no death lets me die. Shock inside shock, burning concatenation of carnage and deceit. Each death links me to a history of deaths—those that are mine and not my own. Faces of cruelty unmasked. My God, this is my lineage. This is the poisoned soil from which I grew. My father, Hyman, is here and his father and his and on and on. Fathers who wreaked their merciless havoc on the world.

A chain of generals, conquerors, CEOs, con men, tyrants, thieves, exploiters of every kind and fools. They die and die here again for all eternity. These are my fathers. These are the men. Allegiance our highest calling. Obedience outweighs logic, morality, or sense. They have called me here. Urging me to cut this foolishness with you and retake my place in the righteous male hierarchy. How wholly absurd. To be zapped over and over like a programmed machine for eternity in order to prove my strength and worth.

I ask you, Eve, what then is the alternative? What is a man cast out of the kingdom of men? Perhaps you cannot understand this loyalty. It's what gives us purpose and meaning and place. What land will we walk on after exile? Adam disobeyed once and we know what that delivered us.

I could stop here. My confessions have already improved my karmic disposition. This dark hell realm is certainly more bearable than the previous limbo. At least there is the sensation of ongoing pain and the motion of repeated dying. And unlike limbo, I am not alone here in this dark room of the fathers.

And I am sure, Eve, this is what I deserve.

But I am conflating the exercise. You bade me here to make an apology. I promised to make the most thorough accounting I could. I did not say I would stop if I landed in a more bearable position. I am doing what I did while

I was alive. Bargaining, manipulating, holding my own interests above all else. Habits die slow.

This apology is a much more grueling and impugning task than I had imagined. The closer one gets to it, the further away it becomes. Each admission begs a deeper accounting; each reckoning has another embedded inside it. It is most certainly a Pandora's box, but these are wrongs already unleashed upon the world. They hang there unaccounted for like ominous and poisonous clouds in the collective psyche. It becomes more and more evident that the story that isn't visible, told, or owned is the one that holds the most power.

Each admission here defies a blood vow determined long before my birth. An apologist is a traitor of the highest order. How many men, how many fathers ever admit to failures or offenses? The act itself is a betrayal of the basic code. It sprays shrapnel of guilt in all directions. If one of us is wrong, the whole structure and story come tumbling down. Our silence is our bond. The power of not telling, of not letting on, is the most ancient and powerful weapon in our arsenal. But there are other techniques that are offered in our basic training manual. Techniques that are in some ways more effective and long-lasting than any physical damage.

Techniques that I used to cause you to doubt your experience, your perceptions, and your worth. How many times did I convince you, in the act of greatest cruelty and violation, that what you were experiencing wasn't that bad, that your reactions were exaggerated and extreme? How many times did I insist that what you were experiencing as pain wasn't pain at all? How many times did I blame you for what I was doing? Or tell you I loved you so much that I was throwing you against a wall? Doing this for your own good. How many ways did I intentionally confuse you and wear you down? How many cases did I build against you and how many witnesses and allies did I rally to my cause?

Daily gaslighting. Until the bitter end, I left you with those lingering doubts, which would wake you, breathless in the night. Had you imagined everything? Was it really as terrible as you remembered? Why didn't the others seem disturbed? Why didn't they say anything? Was something wrong with you? Why not just move on? Why call attention to yourself? Why make a big deal? It's just the way things were. Why rattle the cage, upset the nest? He was your father. He did the best he could. This was your family. You were always so difficult. Why can't you just fit in? Always have to be so grandiose. So special. So, he shoved his grown-up fingers in you when you were five? So, he asked your mother to get a knife from the kitchen so he could stab you? So, he made you bleed and choke? So, he threw you down the stairs? You survived. There are far worse things. Get on with it.

I know all this because these are the questions and self-doubts which consumed me. I bequeathed them to you. These are the incertitudes that kept me wanting, in compliance and in step with the fathers' army.

But even at a young age, you broke rank and would not march. In spite of your brokenness, confusion, and doubt, you somehow questioned and fought back. And I see now, it wasn't initially just rage I felt at your defiance. No, it was awe. It was astonishment. How could you, a ten-year-old girl, be brazen enough to challenge the givens? How could you, a mere child, stand alone outside the circle? What spirit lived in you, what grit, what valor? But admiration was something I could not abide in my limited lexicon of emotions and it quickly turned to resentment and jealousy. Yes, Eve, I was jealous of you. I begrudged your audacity. I could not tolerate the inviolable force of rebelliousness, which made you separate and superior. It showcased all the ways I had betrayed myself by aligning with power. It made my weak and willing acquiescence and submission irredeemably apparent.

But more humiliating, you had dared to openly contradict your father. You had asserted yourself as if you were an equal. You had brazenly challenged my supremacy. You, ungrateful brat, had dared to think you might know better. And you had weakened my authority in the presence of my own kingdom, which was my family. You had wronged me, Eve. And there would be no forgiveness.

This sparked the inexorable winds of wrath and until the day I died and even hereafter they have driven and possessed me.

A wrath spurred by pride and grandiosity. A wrath at myself for betraying my conscience. Wrath at the morbid boredom of domestic life, at annoying children who never measured up, at becoming a corporate idiot and machine. A wrath spurred by the repression of a sickening guilt that I had touched you indecently when you were five and the terror of being found out.

A wrath at all the pathetic people in the world who wasted my time and did nothing more than occupy space.

A wrath that tore down buildings and dreams and personalities, blindly and willfully devastating everything in its tracks. Wrath negated my wisdom and intelligence. It sullied my charm. I was no longer a man. I was a storm.

"All nations shall say, Why has the Lord done thus to this land? What does the heat of this great anger mean? Then men shall say, Because they have forsaken the covenant of the Lord God of their fathers, which he made with them when he brought them out of the land of Egypt; For they went and served other gods, and worshipped them, gods whom they knew not, something that was not their portion. And the anger of the Lord was kindled against this land, to bring upon it all the curses that are written in this book; And the Lord rooted them out of their land in anger and in wrath, and in great indignation, and cast them into another land, as it is this day."

I cursed you, Eve, and cast you from my land. I undermined and ignored you. I belittled your ambitions and erased your possibilities. And there was nothing, nothing you could do to win me back.

No plea of your mother's touched my heart. It didn't matter how far you fell, how close to ruin or poverty or death. It didn't matter how much you craved my acknowledgment and support. I invalidated you on every count. And to this day, I don't know how you did it, but after one year at some third-rate women's college, you turned your academic life around and were able to transfer to a prestigious school. Perhaps it was finally being away from me. Perhaps it was the raging impetus to prove me wrong.

When you came home on a break, you were filled with a new brashness and fire. You were discovering your interests and your talents. You declared at dinner you were going to be an artist, a writer. You were not going to take sciences or math, as I had strongly advised you. You were going to study philosophy and literature. Your arrogance and sureness enraged me. (I see now, again, it was jealousy.) Who were you at nineteen to think you had any idea what you wanted or what you needed to study? I asked you how you thought you would make a living writing "poems." You said you would figure it out. I said you would take classes to prepare you to be a lawyer or an accountant. You said you wouldn't. I said if I am paying for it, you will take classes that prepare you for a realistic future. "No, I will not take those classes. I am getting straight A's now. I will get a scholarship. You can keep your money."

Boom! I pulled the chair out from underneath you and lifted it to crash it on your head. And to my shock, you lunged at me, pushed me back until I almost fell. You lifted your fists. "You don't have to support my classes or my dreams, but if you ever touch me again, I will leave this house forever. I promise you." My God, you were willing to die for this? Raise your fists and strike at me? I was staggered and impressed. You had become a viable adversary. I knew then I had to develop more effective and ruthless strategies to delegitimize this fantasy and bring you down. Battle on.

You were accepted early into the top graduate drama school in the country, one out of six places in the class. You came home on a rare visit to share your excitement and enlist my support. You made your case. You would be graduating from college in a few months. You were clear you wanted to go into the theater. This graduate program would provide the best training and offer a network upon graduating. It was a huge deal that you had been accepted. And again, the hyperbole: "Daddy, it is everything!" And looking back, Eve, it probably was.

"I told you years ago, if you wanted to go this route you would go it on your own." "But I can't get a scholarship if you have money." "That's your problem, Eve. You made your choice. It's up to you to figure it out." Right there I thwarted your foolish dream. Or at least that's what I hoped and thought. At your college graduation you were somehow the keynote speaker. As we sat down in a crowd of thousands, I heard people behind us whispering, "I hear there is this radical feminist addressing us." I suddenly realized they were talking about you, my daughter, and in that moment, you were suddenly a stranger. I did not know you. You had gone away from me to school; you had distinguished yourself and made a life. And as much as I wanted to be proud, I could not bear that you dared to be separate. Who were you to go off and chart a path, determine your own existence? Who were you to think your words and opinions were significant enough to hold the attention of this hall? And more worrying, if they would listen to you, wouldn't others? I sat through your speech, but to be honest I did not hear a word you were saying. There you were at twenty-two standing in front of thousands, filled with charisma and strength. The audience was enraptured. You received a standing ovation. And I am utterly revolted to confess that it infuriated me and threw me off balance. I was the one meant to hold center stage. I was the one entitled to command such admiration and authority.

Then, after your speech, something happened that I will never forget. I have rehashed it here in limbo a million times over. I was anxious and disturbed, so I walked outside after your speech to have a smoke. It was a sweltering day in May. The air was thick. You walked out at the exact same moment. I lit your Lucky Strike. I lit mine. Your hands were still shaking. We stood there in silence, just the two of us, as the ceremony was still going on. It was as if the world had conspired to join us in this suspended moment. A perfect moment for me to praise you, to recognize your stunning achievement. And I knew, I truly knew you had in many ways done this for me, to get my approval and recognition. To show me that you had measured up, that in fact you were not lazy and stupid. And if I could take that moment back right now, I would. For I know my behavior was ruinous.

I stood there, stoic, cold, looking away, utterly indifferent and silent as if nothing had just happened, as if I might even have missed it.

And I could feel you then, Eve. It would be a lie to say I didn't. I knew what you needed from me and I knew even then it would make all the difference for you in that glorious moment and in the years that came after. It would be a turning point when you were finally able to step into yourself, take charge of your destiny.

It was hinged simply on my humble willingness to acknowledge and celebrate you.

But I could not, would not give you that. I would not help you on your way. I needed to keep my claws in you. I needed to dominate and punish. So I said absolutely

nothing. Nothing. Not one word. The silence was stag-
gering. I had already cut off one main avenue for your
future by refusing to give you a penny for graduate
school. There and then I negated your speaking performance by withholding my approval. But the denoue-
ment was diabolical. As we stood there in that sinking
sauna of punishing muteness, I slowly reached into my
pocket. I handed you an envelope with a check inside.
A thousand dollars. I handed it to you, shook your hand
as if you were some corporate client and this were the
completion of a business deal. I looked you blankly in
the eye and without a trace of affection or care, I said,
"Have a good life, Eve." End of story. My obligations
were fulfilled. You want to be a big shot on the stage,
well, now you're on your own. It was a gut punch to your
future. Your knees buckled. You held back the tears. You
turned without saying a word and walked away. To be
honest, you never looked back. Rather than end the war,
I dropped a close-range missile and leveled you.

You got very drunk that night. You were a mess and
a public embarrassment. Your mother said that on a day
you should have been dancing on clouds, you cried yourself to sleep. This moment would forever shatter your
confidence. Every victory thereafter would be glazed
with rejection. No accomplishment would ever be real

or enough, every achievement forever fraught with a dreaded sense of betrayal and disappointment. I know, because I launched that bomb with that particular target and intention. I did that, Eve. I wanted you to fail. I wanted you to fall. I did not want you to succeed at anything.

Your mother could not understand this. Why, she would ask, would you spend all that money on Eve's college education and then undermine her consistently? It made no sense. But there was a fiendish logic. The more independent you became, the more successful, the less control I had of you. You would become your own person then, with your own ideas and your particular version of reality. The more reliable and respected you became, the more possibility there was that you would be a trustworthy witness.

I knew by then that those nightmarish invasions in the dark had ravaged and destroyed you, and I knew you were defiant and rebellious. It was only a matter of time before you would get even. Or this is how my paranoid brain imagined it. I needed to disable you.

Who was I punishing, Eve, who was I trying to destroy?

All along, I made you feel like you were the one who had done something terribly wrong. Always anxious, in an ongoing state of unnamable guilt and dread, I made you the carrier of your father's sin. You carried it like a warrior. You carried it like a wound. You carried it like a mutated cell that later became illness. You carried it like a scarlet letter imprinted on your defiled body, like a sign that you were disposable and forgotten. You carried it like an invitation to waiting predators to inflict more harm. You carried it like an omen that you would not live to be thirty. You almost drank yourself to death, putting yourself in constant danger, secretly dreaming that someone would take you out, stop the pain, undo the curse. And I watched and let it happen.

After college, there was no structure there to support you. You fell from those heady heights. You weren't giving speeches anymore. You lost your voice, your purpose, and your way. I never stepped in to help you and I prohibited your mother from doing so. We visited you once in a sorrowful apartment in New York and the only positive thing I noted was it didn't have rats. When your mother implored me to give you a hand, I railed at her and said you had to make it on your own. I insisted that that was the only way children find their way in the world.

In your deepest economic distress, I never offered you a penny. When you would call at four in the morning in a drunken, suicidal state, I forced your mother to hang up and would not allow her to call to see if you were alive the next day. And for a while you disappeared into the city, swallowed in descending nights of debauchery, danger, and despair. We heard rumors that you were waitressing at a Mafia joint, always drunk, lost on the streets, never awake before one in the afternoon. I was told you were dating a hit man.

Was I hoping you would simply disappear or die? I certainly behaved that way. I hear you crying out—*What kind of father could have allowed his daughter to descend to this? What kind of wrath, of rage, could carry on so long? There must be more to this story. What were you getting out of this?*

Here's the horrid truth, Eve. It gave me pleasure to watch you grovel without money, respect, or a future. It amused me to see you fall from such willful heights chasing an impractical and grandiose future you had independently designed. What business did you have imagining you could be a writer or an artist when I had spent my best years as a high-end ice cream salesman to pay your bills? No Torah, no Plato, nothing to show for my dreams.

And this, I am afraid, opens a much more disturbing can of worms. I had become a person who derived pleasure from your suffering. Prince Charming had devolved into the Marquis de Sade.

As you fell, Eve, I could feel better about myself. You were no longer a threat to my ego or worth. You had betrayed and disobeyed me. You had cast me off and I soaked in satisfaction as the world, in concert with my assessment, dished out your punishment.

I reveled in knowing that you were nothing without me or my endorsement. I took deepest pleasure in proving you could no longer touch my heart. For what is sadism but tenderness disgraced?

And wasn't this my emotional legacy to you—the desecration of your trust, the perversion of your central instinct to be kind? The transmission of this sadistic pleasure and these cruel impulses into the very makeup of your nature? I have often asked myself why you never had children. Did you fear these same urges in you? A teasing that goes on too long, an inner relief when they fall or fail, a sudden inexplicable smack or push, a child accidentally falling down the stairs.

After years, you finally came to visit, and you were newly sober. You were bloated, anxious, and extremely fragile. You had found a "community" and they were helping you. You spoke in absurd clichés and platitudes and spouted rubbish of a "higher power." We were a nonreligious family and I found this departure particularly disturbing. I loathed cults and crutches. I despised groups of any kind. But I could sense a new resolve in you. You had found a raft and were holding on for dear life.

And instead of celebrating this new determination, I made fun of your sobriety, refused to believe or acknowledge you were an alcoholic, disparaged these pathetic losers you were now calling friends. And then, to evidence my condescension and disapproval, I mixed a martini and handed it to you. You were clearly shocked but quietly refused. I laughed at you and tempted you further, and when you held your ground, I said how sad it was that your life, at such a young age, had come to this.

But something had changed in you. You didn't react or even try to defend yourself. You sipped a Tab and kept smoking and smoking. This rattled and provoked me further. You were suddenly out of my grasp. You weren't taking the bait. You were with a group now with greater influence and they had clearly armed you with tactics to resist me. I was furious. I asked you what you were doing with your life. I drilled you and drilled you. I told you I had spent a fortune on your college education and you had succeeded at nothing. You were a waitress with no vision or plan. What a failure you had become. You did not say a word. You said you needed to make a call and left the room. When you returned, your bag was packed. You said that this environment had become threatening to your sobriety, that that was your priority, and then you were gone. It all happened so fast. You cut the cord that was choking you and walked out the door. And that severing sent me spinning. I was flabbergasted and insane. Who were you to walk out of my house, to claim a priority and way of life outside my purview? Who were you to take your life into your own hands? I know this sounds utterly bizarre in retrospect, but even in the midst of this endless time of wrath, you somehow still belonged to me; as long as you were disabled and drunk, I would own you. As long as you were a mess, you would need my approval and validation.

I grow sick of these horrific confessions and myself. Rattling and oinking on and on. Stuck like an unctuous pig spinning on a torturous spit of gangrenous self-centeredness. God, let me out of me. Break this impossible shell. Free me from this netherworld of endless mirrors. Have I even come close to touching the layer of veracity and admission that would free you? For it seems to me that an apology insists on a most primal intimacy.

And if the confession is a request for forgiveness, the confessor must be stripped and laid bare.

I see now that this exercise is not simply a relaying of regrets. No, implicit in an apology is a reimagining of the basic constructs of our conditioning. And I sense I am failing. Even now, I wonder if the walls of my imperiousness allow me to truly see or feel you. Have I even stopped to consider or intuit what kind of ruptures and suffering these brutal acknowledgments are causing in you? Are you relieved, or shocked? Are you enraged? Are you sleepless and bereft? Are you finally vindicated and on fire?

And how would I know this? Do you even exist beyond the gates of myself? Are you a figment, a projection, an extension? Are you a target or a threat or a perennial resentment? My God, Eve, I am ashamed to say I do not know you. Well, I know you fancied marinated mushrooms and herring and dill pickles, but only because I fancied them. But I have no idea what books you read, what poems were your guides through life. Did you read Nietzsche, Emerson, Baudelaire? What kind of friends were you drawn to? What was a life in the theater like? Did you ever perform? Were you really a lesbian? Did you ever develop an appetite? Are you an ocean person, or do you prefer the woods and mountains? Why did you really become a vegetarian? What was the bravest thing you ever did? Are you funny? Did you move to the city because of me? Should I have brought you up as a Jew? Are you a morning person? Do you prefer roses to peonies? Did you have cats? Do you pray or believe in God? Do you drink coffee or tea? How did it work out with your adopted son? Did you ever make money?

Who are you, Eve? I missed everything. I missed you. I miss you.

I refused to know or see you. And this in some ways was the most destructive and punishing deprivation. Isn't that all any us crave, really? To be known? To be given shape and form by being recognized and cherished? For how else can we trust that we are even here? And perhaps that is why I became so extreme. Because I was invisible to myself, because I had been erased, I needed to find ways to experience my existence and feel my impact on others. For what is violence but energy given substance and force?

And I knew that from a very young age you were troubled deeply by this same kind of existential angst. I was surprised and a bit disturbed this had come to occupy you so early, but now of course it makes much sense. You were constantly obsessing about death, asking questions about what your body would become, where you would go, would you completely just evaporate one day, disintegrate and disappear?

One night when you were about nine or ten years old, your mother and I had been out for dinner and we came home to find the babysitter sitting outside the bathroom on the floor. She was a teenager and was clearly disturbed. You had watched a movie called *The Invisible Man* with Claude Rains which was way too mature for your years. You were inside, your head over the toilet, vomiting and crying, in a kind of spiritual despair, trying to catch your breath, hardly making sense: "He unwrapped the bandages around his head, Daddy, and nothing was there, there was nothing inside, no head, no person, nothing there. Where did he go? Was he ever here? Is there anything really inside our bodies? Do we even exist? Are we nothing? I feel like nothing, I don't want to be nothing." And then you would cry and vomit more. This went on for two days, as if you were consumed by an existential fever.

And now I am compelled to ask, who made you nothing? I have no excuses, as I knew too well the devastating consequences of not being seen, of disappearing in a family that never expressed any curiosity about who I really was, but determined my identity based on their own projections, fears, and needs. Curiosity is a form of generosity. Implicit in it is the recognition of another, requiring the puncturing of the vain inglorious shell of self-importance. Did anyone ever really exist but me? Did I experience or feel or perceive anyone outside myself? Did I know wonder?

As a child I was awed by sky and stars and the magnificence of creation. But all that was quickly discouraged and directed into performance. There was no time to linger in idle meditation. I was here like other boys to improve myself, to achieve, advance, and win. This world of mystery and wonder was not to be appreciated and revered. It was to be occupied, owned, and conquered.

Implicit in wonder is humility. To surrender to what is larger and unknown, to that vast, mysterious universe of which you are a tiny dot. I was not allowed to be a tiny part of anything. I had to be above, the best, on top.

I remember I must have been about five years old when I experienced a baby sparrow in my hand (it had fallen from a tree), felt its tiny heart beating in my five-year-old fist. My heart was beating just as fast. Who made this bird? Who thought up wings and beaks and claws? Did he get in trouble with his mother? Did she throw him on the ground? Was it an accident? Is he sad? Is he broken? Why can't he fly? Will he teach me how?

I was stunned, terrified, in awe. It was almost unbearable having him so intimately there in my hand, but I could not, would not let go. I was in possession of a miracle. I had the secret to the universe wrapped in my knuckle. All time stopped. I was bird. I was rapture taken in the invisible current of awe. I was everything and all.

And then I was suddenly and rudely awakened, my mother screaming in fright. "What are you doing, Arthur? Get that dirty bird out of your hand. They carry terrible diseases. You are disgusting." She shook me hard and knocked the bird out of my hand. He went tumbling and landed badly on the ground. He didn't move after that and I was not allowed to help or go near him.

It was more than I could bear, and I burst out crying. I cried and cried, and this was the greatest lapse of all. To cry and show weakness. This was worse than being lost in awe and surrender to a baby bird.

And what, you ask, is a life without wonder? It is drab and dreary. It is one of imposed certainty and compulsory routine. It is devoid of splendor and excitement with a bolted doorway to astonishment.

So what, then, becomes of men's passion and intensity? It is rerouted early on into dominance, aggression, and competition.

Which leads me to the contempt and cruelty I lodged at your first husband. Suddenly, after years of not visiting, you brought home a man whom you were planning to marry. A thick Irish Catholic fellow who could hardly spell. A bartender you met in some classless joint where you waitressed. A scoundrel at best. Maybe an embezzler or a thief. (Well, there was no evidence of that, but I treated him as such.)

Your mother said he was handsome and charming, but to me your choice felt as arbitrary as bringing home a stray dog you had found on the street. There was no conversation to be had with him. But did I try? I did not. His sudden existence was a most annoying intrusion. It was clear the only reason you were marrying him was to get back at me. He was everything I was not. Uneducated, rough, uncouth, and sober. Yet even though I detested this lout, I immediately set forth to make him my ally. At dinner, I told him you appeared to be one thing but you were really another. I thought it was best he be prepared and know what he was getting himself into. I acted as a man protector even though I had no interest in him at all. Then I gleefully regaled him with intimate details of your willful transgressions. I told him the terrible things you had done as a child and teenager; implicit in each was your questionable character.

I complained that you were the most impossible child and had provoked me to behavior contrary to my nature.

I embraced him as a brother soldier in my army to defeat you. Even your mother was horrified by this. You were caught off guard, humiliated and furious. I was planting seeds of doubt in the man you were marrying— showcasing your lowly disposition and outlining your failures. This went on for almost an hour. At first you kept laughing, trying to deflect what I was saying and to move the conversation in another direction. But I would not be deterred. I went on and on with a vengeance until I delivered the final blow. I told him I had had to wash my hands of you, and I would understand, after hearing all this, if he needed to back out too.

But the wedding somehow went on.

I see you now at twenty-three, standing at a home-made altar in a flimsy white dress you had found in an upscale store on a sales rack for torn items, at a wedding haphazardly arranged by begging and borrowing. I had refused to pay. There were only cheap hors d'oeuvres and there was no hard liquor. Standing there surrounded by a ragtag collection of friends and struggling artists, in a service performed by a hokey minister from a religion I'd never heard of in which he never mentioned God. I see you marrying a man whose most compelling feature was that he hadn't hit you. I hear you making some inexplicable mishmash of vows which failed to include faithfulness. (I know now that it never occurred to you to expect or demand it.) I see you standing with a teenage boy, son of your husband-to-be, whom you had committed to adopting and mothering. You were somehow giving him what you needed most.

There is a black man dressed in African garb playing a saxophone—a sorrowful melody, more fitting for a funeral than a wedding. That music comes to me now, a woeful wail, as I begin to walk you down a makeshift aisle. You hold my arm. Maybe the first time you have touched me in years. At first, I had refused to participate in this ludicrous ritual—give you away to this idiot. But then at the last moment something in me relented. In all sincerity, it was the perfect opportunity to reinstate my ownership and authority. And as I walk you step by step through the crowd of wedding onlookers, I am horrified to say I took great satisfaction in knowing that this marriage was already doomed.

You had chosen a man who was married when you met him. I think you were number three. And even if you appeared to share great humor (you were endlessly laughing together, which annoyed me deeply) and were able to find comfort and structure in your mutual sobriety,

I knew he could not and would not be honest or loyal to you.

But more importantly I know this wedding is entirely a sham as you are still married to me. I grip your arm harder. We made a silent covenant in the dark when you were just five. Even if you share your body with this oaf, he will never really touch you. He will never feel the triumph and sacredness of discovering ecstasy because you've already had it. He will never enter the room of the beloved because I occupy it. And this will eventually drive him (and all the others that come after) to anger and distraction—this sense that he can never really have you.

At first, he will be drawn to it as a challenge. Every man loves a battle. But then, after time, it will make him feel empty, stupid, and a failure. And when he realizes you are never going to give yourself to him, even though you pretend you did, he will retaliate and do all he can to hurt you. Punch holes in walls, betray you with other women, eventually leave you for your close friend. These were the toxic thoughts I circulated in the vulnerable atmosphere of your already penurious wedding. This was the crippling energy I pressed like invisible poison into your skin as I gripped your arm. This was your father not calmly and kindly walking you down the aisle to meet your beloved, but instead your predator scheming and marching you to your inevitable slaughter.

The saxophone, louder now, is wailing and screeching. Waves of sound crashing against these sodden walls. Oh grief, typhoon of grief. Spinning and smashing me on guilt-edged crags and rocks, tangled in endless wreckage and debris. It has me now, this grief. The waves blow back. This is the piercing. The man shell cracking. What kind of bastard have I been? What kind of destruction have I wrought? I have lied and lied to myself and you.

I cursed your future of love. At five I took your body. You didn't give it to me. I contaminated your sweetness. I ripped the protective golden gates from your garden. I betrayed your trust. I rearranged your sexual chemistry and the basis of your desire. Wrongness and excitement were forever fused together. I made my stain. I left my stinking mark. I infected you. By invading and over-whelming your body I killed your yearning so early. You did not and could not give me permission. There was no consent. You did not seduce me with your crino-line petticoats. You were simply being an adorable child.

I overstimulated your five-year-old body and planted the seeds of intensity and thrill. You would push your-self too far, take heroin, jump off bridges, drive a hundred miles an hour.

I robbed you of the ordinary. I destroyed your notion of family. I forced you to betray your mother. You lived in perpetual self-hatred and guilt. I created hierarchy, distrust and violent competition between you and your siblings. None of you would recover from this.

I robbed you of agency over your body. You didn't make any decisions. You didn't say yes. That was my projection in order to satisfy my needs. You were five years old. I was fifty-two. You had no sovereignty. I exploited and abused you. I took your body. It was no longer yours. I rendered you passive. You compulsively gave it to whoever wanted it because I taught you you should. I forced you out of your body, and because you were dislocated and numb, you were unable to protect yourself. I compromised your safety and ability to defend yourself. I made it so that rape became what turned you on. I eviscerated your necessary boundaries so you never knew what was yours and when to say no or how to say stop. I tore the delicate walls of your vagina and made it vulnerable to disease and infection.

Your body didn't and couldn't say yes. This was a convenient lie I told myself. You didn't know it was sex. I took what I needed by convincing myself you needed it too. I exploited your adoration. I forced you into secrecy, to lie to your mother, to develop a dual life. This split you in two. I made you feel like a whore. I made you feel you were never worthy of legitimate love. I made intimacy claustrophobic. I left my poison in you.

I destroyed your memory by making you want to forget everything. This impacted your intelligence and ability to contain facts and take tests. I stole your innocence. I dimmed your life force and made you feel your sexuality was the cause of bad things. I used your being and body to serve myself.

I did all this. Oh saxophone, take me out. Take me out.

Slowly, painfully, I crawl like a weatherbeaten crab out of the now quiet and retreating sea. I collapse on warm sand. I lie there exhausted and broken. I am there for days or months or years. I am formed again. I feel myself. My clothes are gone. So is my sex. I have little breasts and shorter legs and smaller feet. My stomach is supple. There are two moles above my left eye. This is your face, Eve. This is your body. I am inside it. I notice blood.

My nose is bleeding. My neck is sore. There are bruises from being choked. My rear end stings from the paddle. There are welts on my thighs. Scars and wounds surfacing like leprous lumps all over me. I am the wound and the wound maker. I am burning.

I roll on the sand, hurl myself into the sea. The salty water irritates and aggravates the cuts and injuries. My vagina is on fire, I hold it and rock and scream and cry out and it is your agonized little-girl voice that comes out of my mouth. "Make it stop. Make it stop."

The beach is empty and vast, not a bird, not a sound. Does anyone know I am here? Does anyone care? A voice pounding in my head: "No one is coming. No one is coming." And a trap door opens, and I fall in. I fall and fall into the void, the absence, into the limbo of the dispossessed.

I am nothing. I have no family. I have no place. I have no father. I have no mother. I am badness. I am shame. I am disgraced.

Oh God, Eve, I now see, I have been spinning for thirty-one years in the torturous limbo I made inside you, in the terrible cavern of loneliness that nothing or no one could fill, in the desperate abyss of your waiting.

Oh, what is happening now? What slivers of light are breaking through this dark? What glimmering demarcations? Stars. Stars. Millions of them. I am so grateful for the stars.

Each one is a shining little face, leaning out to be noticed or cherished or seen. Expectant eyes and ready cheeks. Each one performing sparkling tricks hoping to be adopted or redeemed. Each star is a luminous child who got missed.

Eve,
Let me say these words:
I am sorry. I am sorry. Let me sit here at the final hour. Let me get it right this time. Let me be staggered by your tenderness. Let me risk fragility. Let me be rendered vulnerable. Let me be lost. Let me be still. Let me not occupy or oppress. Let me not conquer or destroy. Let me bathe in the rapture. Let me be the father.
Let me be the father who mirrors your kindheartedness back to you. Let me lay no claims. Let me bear witness and not invade.

Eve,
I free you from the covenant. I revoke the lie. I lift the curse.
Old man, be gone.

ACKNOWLEDGMENTS

I could not have written this book without beloved friend Michael Klein, my husky-voiced midwife who saw what I was doing when I could not and had faith when I was too anxious to breathe. Thank you for the depth of your listening and invaluable insights and just being there, being there.

Thank you, Johann Hari, for your time, your precious insights, and for staying with me through the tricky passage. Thank you, Sue Grand, for giving me a way to name and frame the terror and dread, for so many years of insights that freed me from hell.

Thank you, James Lecesne, for being the best friend ever and believing so deeply, and Monique Wilson for your constancy, kindness, and deep love. Paula Allen for listening and knowing, my mama angel Carole Black for your mentorship and guidance, and Jennifer Buffett for journeying with me and through our travels making this book possible.

Thank you to Christine Schuler Deschryver, my brave and beautiful friend, and all my sisters in Bukavu who teach me daily how to turn pain into power.

Thank you to the circle of astounding friends and colleagues whose love and brilliance is both protection and inspiration: Rada Borić, Pat Mitchell, Diana de Vegh, Arundhati Roy, Jane Fonda. Naomi Klein, Thandie Newton, Laura Flanders, Kimberlé Crenshaw, Alixa Garcia, Nicoletta Billi. Zillah Eisenstein, Elizabeth Lesser, David Stone, Diane Paulus, Diane Borger, Ryan McKittrick, George Lane, Nancy Rose, Frank Selvaggi, Harriet Clark, Zoya, Adisa Krupalija, Peter Buffett, Mark Matousek, Rosa Clemente, Tony Porter, Ted Bunch, and Farah Tanis.

My astonishing V-Day team: Susan Swan, Purva Panday Cullman, Carl Cheng, Leila Radan, Anju Kasturiraj, Kristina Shea, (Mo and Mama C). Thank you for rocking this global movement and teaching me every day what solidarity and collaboration looks like.

Thank you my precious son, Dylan McDermott, daughter, Maggie Q, and my astounding bubbe girls, Coco McDermott and Charlotte McDermott. You are my heart.

Tony Montenieri for everything you do that allows me to write and for the kindness enfolded in every act.

I am so deeply grateful to my brilliant editor Nancy Miller for her radiant belief in this book, her superb and careful editing, and for pushing me to go deeper.

Bless the wonderful team at Bloomsbury and Emi Battaglia.

Thank you, Steven Barclay and Eliza Fischer and all the wonderful ones at the Barclay Agency.

I am particularly grateful to Charlotte Sheedy, my agent extraordinaire of forty-two years. I bow in gratitude to your constancy, your belief in my work, your loyalty, and your fierce fighting ways. I love you.

I want to acknowledge my brother, Curtis, for the immensity of his heart, for surviving what we survived, for sharing a history and memories that begged an apology.

For all the thousands of women I have met over these last twenty-plus years in refugee camps, hospitals, war zones, prisons, plays, centers, colleges, high schools, safe houses, places of worship who generously shared your stories and inspire me every day to keep fighting until our daughters are equal, free, and safe.

For all the men who have hurt women, may this book inspire you to do your own deep and thorough accounting, reckoning, apologizing so that we can finally transform and end this violence.

A NOTE ON THE AUTHOR

EVE ENSLER is a Tony Award–winning playwright, author, performer, and activist. She wrote the international bestselling phenomenon *The Vagina Monologues*, which won an Obie, has been published in 48 languages, and has been performed in more than 140 countries. She is the author of many plays and books, including the *New York Times* bestseller *I Am an Emotional Creature*. She recently adapted her highly praised memoir *In the Body of the World* into a play, which ran to critical acclaim at the American Repertory Theater and Manhattan Theatre Club. Her play *The Vagina Monologues* gave birth to V-Day, a global activist movement to end gender-based violence. Through benefit productions of her artistic works, the V-Day movement has raised more than $100 million and funded more than 13,000 community-based anti-violence programs and safe houses throughout the world. She is also the founder of One Billion Rising, the largest global mass action campaign to combat violence against women and girls. Ensler is a co-founder, along with Christine Schuler Deschryver and 2018 Nobel Peace Prize winner Dr. Denis Mukwege, of the City of Joy, a revolutionary center for women survivors of violence in the Democratic Republic of the Congo. She was named one of *Newsweek*'s 150 Women Who Changed the World and one of the *Guardian*'s 100 Most Influential Women. She lives in New York.